The Disappearance of Kemberly Ramer

Pete Dove

Published by Trellis Publishing, 2021.

THE DISAPPEARANCE OF KEMBERLY RAMER

First edition. July 11, 2021.

ISBN: 979-8223484721

Written by Pete Dove.

The Disappearance of Kemberly RAMER

PETE DOVE

JASMINE RICHARDSON

On the South Saskatchewan River in Alberta, Canada is a town called Medicine Hat. With a population of just over 60,000 it is filled with little communities where everybody knows everybody. With a relatively low crime rate and virtually none of those crimes involving homicide it's the perfect place to raise a family in a safe environment, or at least it would seem that way I should I say. The security offered by Medicine Hat was greatly diminished when the entire town was shaken to its core in April of 2006.

On April 23, 2006 the community was rocked to its very foundation with the discovery of a gruesome triple homicide. An entire family was found stabbed to death in their home that day. The bodies were discovered by the 8 year old boy's best friend when he arrived at the house to get his friend to come out and play. When cops were notified and an investigation began the scene revealed was one of the worst scenes in Canadian history. Debra Richardson, 48 and her husband Marc, 42 were found in the basement with multiple stab wounds covering their bodies and upon further investigation their son 8 year old Jacob was found also stabbed to death with his throat slit in his bed upstairs. Such a horrific scene was left behind that the police responding would be affected long after the investigation. It didn't take police long to realize that family photos around the home depicted a family of 4 instead of 3. The 12 year old daughter Jasmine was missing. Immediately police were concerned that they had a kidnapping on their hands. The sweet angelic looking daughter in the photos must have been victimized by the monster that did this to her family as well. However, the sweet loving family photos that the police encountered depicting a 12 year old girl were not the reality where Jasmine was concerned. Jasmine had started acting and dressing differently. She had new friends, she was getting in trouble and going off to wild parties and she had a 23 year old boyfriend that her parents detested here being with. That boyfriend was into drugs, drinking, and dark things like werewolves, vampires, and the Goth culture. In fact that boyfriend even claimed to be a werewolf himself and reportedly professed to liking the taste of blood. Jasmine Richardson was not missing because she had been kidnapped rather she was missing because she was responsible. It would be later discovered that Jasmine and her 23 year old boyfriend, Jeremy Steinke had committed the murders themselves and had gone on the run.

Background

Once upon a time Jasmine Richardson was the sweet little girl depicted in the family photos around the Richardson house. Once upon a time the family was the perfect poster family for suburban bliss but something went wrong. Jasmine became interested in the Goth culture as well as the Wiccan religion. With this interest came a dark side to the little girl.

At 12 the little girl looked much older; perhaps 15 or 16 and she even claimed to be that old on social media. Soon she had the attention of local man Jeremy Steinke. Jasmine and Jeremy fell into a dangerous relationship. They idolized a life of negativity. They dressed in dark fantasy type clothing and they frequented sites on the internet like vampire freaks, a social media site for teens that love all things vampire. In fact Jeremy himself claimed to love the taste of blood and that he was a 300 year old werewolf. Jeremy had more practice at the twisted lifestyle that they both began to lead than Jasmine did but he was also weakened by a controlling effect that Jasmine had on him. Jasmine knew how to manipulate Jeremy. In many ways this seemed to spell love for Jeremy; he had found a girl that he would do anything for. In Jasmine's case Jeremy was an adult that she could control. She might have to live under what felt like the tyranny of her parents and she might have to go by the rules at the strict Catholic school that she attended but with Jeremy she had the say so. She could only wish for something and Jeremy was there to try to make her wishes come true. This might all sound like the musings of a warped but innocent mind, a reality created by dissatisfied kids looking to feel like they have more control over their lives but Jasmine and Jeremy took things much farther than most kids would dare to go. Just like any good loving parents the Richardsons became alarmed when they learned of the changes in their daughter's lifestyle. The most alarming thing to Jasmine's parents was Jeremy. No parent is going to be comfortable with their 12 year old little girl being in a relationship with a 23 year old man. More alarmingly their relationship was sexual as well. Jasmine may have looked much older but she still had the mind and body of a 12 year old girl chronologically speaking.

When Jasmine told Jeremy online that she had a plan to kill her family he hopped on board. They wrote instant messages to each other discussing the killing of Jasmine's family. Below are the exact words they typed to each other in a snippet of their conversation.

Jasmine: "I have this plan. It begins with me killing them and ends with me living with you."

Jeremy: "I love your plan but we need to get a little more creative with like details and stuff."

Who knows now if either of them were truly serious about committing the murders in the beginning but in the end Jeremy got pumped up watching the movie *Natural Born Killers,* got drunk, did some lines of cocaine and then he was ready to help his beloved carry out her request to alleviate herself of her bothersome parents. All it took was a set of loving protective parents trying to protect their 12 year old daughter from the psychological and perhaps even physical damage that would come from having a sexual relationship with a 23 year old man and Jasmine and Jeremy were all too ready to put an end to the two nuisances trying to keep them apart.

On the night of April 22nd Jeremy watched *Natural Born Killers* with his friends, did some drinking and drugs and then he was ready. He would do anything to make Jasmine happy. Despite her young age and the considerable age gap between the two Jasmine knew how to manipulate Jeremy. Jeremy snuck into the basement of The Richardson's split level home and waited. Thinking she heard noises Debra Richardson, already in her night gown, went down to investigate. She couldn't have been prepared for what awaited her. As soon as Debra flipped on the light switch Jeremy attacked her stabbing her 12 times before killing her. Debra's husband Marc was close behind after hearing the commotion and armed with a screwdriver. However, in the end his screwdriver was no match for Jeremy's knife. Later Jeremy would tell an undercover police officer that he was worried Marc would get the better of him and that Marc nearly succeeded in defending himself with that screwdriver. No matter the fight Marc put up the scene ended up with him on the floor still in a defensive stance, dead with 24 stab wounds. Later Jeremy would say that Marc asked 'why' just before he died and Jeremy replied, 'it's what your daughter wanted.'

After killing Marc and Debra Jeremy headed upstairs leaving a trail of blood in his wake. Upstairs Jasmine was trying to calm her little brother down. At this point Jeremy and Jasmine's stories are not the same. Both of them say it was the other that actually killed the little boy. I suppose we will never know the truth nevertheless young Jacob was found in his bed with stab wounds in his body and his throat slit side to side. Jasmine and Jeremy left the scene and reportedly went back to a friend's apartment to have sex after obliterating Jasmine's entire family. They were the outlaw lovers that they had dreamed of being bound together even more so by the horrific blood bath they had just caused. The two went on the run but they didn't make it far. After a search of Jasmine's school locker a graphic picture surfaced of a girl's whole family burning in a fire while she laughs and escapes with her boyfriend. When police saw this drawing they went from searching for Jasmine as a victim to searching for her as a suspect.

Jasmine and Jeremy were apprehended in Saskatchewan the very next day after the bodies of her family were discovered. The pair were reportedly laughing and joking around with friends about the murders only one day after they had taken place.

Unfathomable Murder

The Richardsons were the picturesque family living in a picturesque neighborhood. Ross Glen, the community where the Richardsons lived, was a middle class neighborhood full of working class families. Their neighbors on one side were Sara and her six year old son Gareth, Jacob's best friend, and their neighbors on the other side were Phyllis and Vernon Gehring. The Gehrings were an elderly couple that liked to garden and look after their dog, a shi tzu Bishon mix. Often the scene would be that Gareth and Jacob could be found playing in the backyard as children do and the Gehrings would delight in tossing balls back over the fence when they strayed a bit too far. The Gehrings felt like Jacob kept them young. They admittedly didn't know much about the daughter. Just the night before that fateful afternoon when the bodies were found Marc Richardson had grilled hot dogs in the backyard for the boys while the Gehring's dog played with the Richardson family's dog through the fence. Everything seemed perfect in that sleepy little neighborhood until that fateful afternoon on April 23rd when Gareth went looking for his best friend.

It was about 1pm and Sara and Gareth had been at Sara's mom's house but Gareth had been asking to play with Jacob all morning. When Gareth could not get anyone to answer the phone at the Richardson residence Sara told him that they could go to the movies. Gareth was still bummed out about not getting to see Jacob and when he and his mom returned home before heading to the movies he darted over to the Richardson's after seeing that Marc's white pickup truck was in the driveway. Gareth knocked on the door but there was no answer, as a curious little boy might he began peering into the basement windows of the split level home. When he saw lifeless bodies and a basement covered in blood he ran back to his mom to tell her what he'd seen. Although Gareth wasn't usually the type of boy to make up stories the things he was saying to Sara just didn't make sense. As she followed him over to the neighbor's house she warned him that he had better not be lying. Sadly Gareth was not lying. When she peered through the same windows that Gareth had Sara saw a horrible scene in front of her. She was afraid that the intruder that had done this was still around, maybe he was even in her house waiting for her and Gareth. She called her mom and her mom told her she had to call 911. Sara's mom and the police headed to the scene. What would unfold at that crime scene would haunt police officers that investigated for years to come. Some of the officers involved were touched so much by young Jacob's defiled body that they broke down on the stand months later when they had to talk about it.

The police came in thinking that they might have an intruder still lurking about the property. They entered with caution. What they saw was unfathomable. There were the bodies of a man and woman in the basement both covered in blood. The woman, Debra Richardson was slumped in the floor with her night gown hiked up exposing the fact that all she had been wearing when she was attacked was that night gown. There was blood all over her and a pool of blood all around her. The little black family dog was standing beside her. Perhaps he felt that he needed to protect her but sadly it was too late for that. Across the basement slumped against a wall was Marc Richardson. His hands were straight out as though he were trying to defend himself. He was frozen by rigor mortis in a defensive state that did nothing for his defense in the end. Marc was wearing only black boxer shorts and a screwdriver was lying beside him. He, too, was riddled with stab wounds. The entire basement was covered in splatters of blood, there had been a real struggle between the Richardsons and their assailant. Upon further investigation of the house the police came across their worst nightmare. The first bedroom was empty but the next bedroom they came to was Jacob's. Jacob was lying in his bed. Police had hope for a moment that the boy was still alive but when they approached they were greeted with the worst. Jacob was in his bed with his throat slashed and stab wounds littering his body as well. There was blood all over his room including many of his toys. A toy light saber was lying in his floor; a useless object against the onslaught of the knife that had ended his life. In the master bedroom the comforter was thrown back as though the bed's occupants had left in a hurry. There was a pillow thrown awkwardly in the floor. Police wondered with horror if the boy had heard his parents being attacked before the assailant ever made it upstairs to him and clutched the pillow trying to find some comfort in the act. As they made another sweep of the house the police noticed that there were four members of the Richardson family instead of three. Instantly everyone's heart sank. A family photo depicted a sweet smiling 12 year old girl and she was nowhere to be found. Police searched that house several times over for either the body of the little girl or perhaps the girl hiding somewhere too afraid to come out after the horrible things she had witnessed but in the end they had to admit defeat, the fourth member of the Richardson family was nowhere to be seen. On the plus side her body wasn't there slain with the rest of her family but the police had to think the worst. The most logical thought was that she may have been kidnapped by whoever did this to her family. And even if she was safe, perhaps spending the night at a friend's house she would still have to deal with the tragic news that she had no family left, that her family had all been brutally attacked and killed. Hearts went out for the girl and for the family she had lost. No one wanted to be left breaking that news to a 12 year old.

The hunt for Jasmine Richardson began, or actually continued, as her parents had reported that she was missing before the terrible crime had ever even taken place. Where was Jasmine? Safe, but oblivious to the fact that this terrible thing had happened to her parents? Scared alone and possibly seriously injured in the hands of the monster that did this to her family? No one could say. As part of the investigation police visited Jasmine's school and got permission to look inside her locker. They were looking for any kind of evidence that would lead them to Jasmine whatsoever but what they found was truly a shocking discovery. When the police searched Jasmine's locker they found a hand drawn picture depicting a horrible scene. In the picture a girl's family burns to death after she puts gasoline in the sprinklers while they have a family picnic. The stick figure girl in the drawing laughs as her family burns and she escapes in her boyfriend's pickup truck. This drawing shifted suspicions entirely and Jasmine Richardson went from being searched for as a victim to being searched for as a suspect in the murder of her parents and her little brother. Consequently it didn't take the police long to track Jasmine and Jeremy down. The pair were said to be joking around with friends about the murders even at the time of apprehension. They were found at a high school in Saskatchewan only about 60 miles from Medicine Hat.

Both Jasmine and Jeremy were jailed and both were convicted. Because of Jasmine's young age at the time under Canadian law she had to be referred to as JR instead of her name. She also was protected from being tried as an adult. Although she got the maximum sentence for a child her age that sentence was only 10 years and under the conditions the time she had already spent in jail counted toward her 10 years. She ended up being imprisoned under the conditions of 4 years locked up undergoing rehabilitation and 4.5 years under very close supervision in the community. Jeremy, on the other hand, was 23 years old at the time of the murders. He was found guilty of three counts of first degree murder and sentenced to three life sentences to be served consecutively. An undercover officer rode with Jeremy while he was being transported from one facility to the other. In the conversation the two had together Jeremy expressed that he loved Jasmine more than anything and that the kind of thing he did was the kind of thing that truly expressed that love. He admitted to everything he did in such a straight forward way that it seemed he did not even grasp the gravity of the situation. He even shared his plans to marry Jasmine when they were both able to get out of prison. On murderpedia.org you can actually read the transcript of the conversation that Jeremy had with the undercover officer that he believed to be another prison being transported along with him. Steinke will be eligible for parole after 25 years.

Some of the residents of Medicine Hat were actually outraged with the outcome of the trial. They didn't think that justice would be served with Jasmine getting away with such little time. Wayne Chopek is one such resident that has spoken out about his outrage. Wayne was a friend of the family and he is disgusted at the fact that Jasmine would go free after a short ten years. However, the law remains the law and in Canada the government believes that children as young as Jasmine was at the time of the murders need to be rehabilitated rather than being locked up and having the key thrown away. They believe that such young lives have more potential value than to doom them to the rest of their lives behind bars.

Life After Murder

After Jasmine and Jeremy were arrested and jailed they still held onto the flame that was recklessly burning before the murders. They were not able to have any contact with one another except for letter writing so they wrote back and forth. This is how Jeremy came to ask Jasmine to marry him and she said yes. Below is an excerpt of the letters passed between the two when Jeremy popped the question.

Jeremy: "Without you this life isn't worth living... U said you want to get engaged? Then here's a Q...Will U marry me? If so then it is a verbal agreement!"

Jasmine: "Ahahaha! I never thought I'd find myself hystericaly laughing in a holding cell in these kinds of circumstances...or ever really. But still! ahaha you make me so happy! Yes! Yes! I will, I would love to... "

Interestingly enough as bright as that flame might have been it eventually flickered out. Although they professed the deepest of bonds neither of the two would admit to actually being the one to Kill Jacob. Both blamed the other. This was one of the deciding factors that actually showed that there were holes in the loving couple's relationship. The two broke up in jail. After incarceration the relationship that had been important enough to kill for dwindled until it was no more.

Perhaps free of any attachment to Jeremy Steinke Jasmine could truly rehabilitate. Jasmine underwent psychiatric evaluations and was determined to be suffering from oppositional defiance disorder as well as conduct disorder. When she first started therapy she was determined to suffer from dependency issues, anxiety and depression. As well as all this she was prone to immature problem solving and wishful fantasies. All this is a lot to bog down a 12 year old but was it enough of a load to excuse the execution of the murder of her entire family? Many say no, some say yes. At any rate it is indeed enough to at least explain some of her behaviors. Once in therapy Jasmine began making progress toward rehabilitation though in the beginning her details of how things played out her a bit skewed to reality. By 2010 Jasmine was making significant progress in her rehabilitation and had professed to be sorry for the crimes she committed. As the terms of her sentencing were laid out she got credit on her sentence for the time she spent in jail awaiting trial and then after 4 years of incarceration she was deemed fit enough to go into the community under very close supervision for 4.5 years. During that time Jasmine was shown to exhibit exemplary behavior as well as being a straight A student. Jasmine was admitted to Calgary University where she continued to earn really high grades. This year, 2016, in May Jasmine became a completely free woman. The courts have no reason to think that she is a danger to society any longer. It's been a decade and she has been through extensive amounts of therapy and shown nothing but progress in that entire time.

A very interesting thing to look at here is the chemistry between Jasmine and Jeremy. One asks themselves, was the combination just toxic? Would either of them been capable of doing something like this on their own? It seems that the pairing of the two and the dependency that both of them exhibited for the other was actual such an explosive combination that it pushed them over the edge just enough to create the perfect circumstance for this to happen. Jasmine has said that she wasn't really being serious when she would send Jeremy messages saying that she had a plan to kill her parents and live with him. That she didn't really mean to go through with it when she joked about murdering her family or made drawings depicting their deaths. But she felt those feelings and she told Jeremy. Steinke just happened to be easily manipulated, a regular user of multiple drugs, and even believed himself to be a 300 year old werewolf. Jeremy and Jasmine both took the dark Goth culture they lived within to the extreme. They exchanged vials of blood and Jeremy wore one around his neck. When the two were faced with Jasmine's parents making them unable to see one another dark fantasies were transformed into evil realities. Perhaps the fantasies that both harbored were purely fantasies until the tension kept rising and rising and the two kept feeding off of each other until the combination of each of their dark thoughts breathed life into the other. In the end it doesn't really matter to ask if either would have been capable of the atrocity on their own because it wasn't the case that they were on their own. They were bound together by an obsessive unhealthy love and the obsessive unhealthy thoughts in both their heads took form in reality. The result was unspeakable horror.

That late April day three lives were lost much too soon and in such a violent way that it is nearly unthinkable. That alone is enough to make this tragedy stand out forever in history but that's not all that was lost. Little Gareth will never be the same. Though he is a successful high schooler now the memory of those bodies and the memory of the loss of his best friend will always be with him. And of course Jasmine Richardson and Jeremy Steinke's lives will forever be changed and affected. Jeremy will most likely spend his entire life in jail having had only 23 short years of freedom. Parole will be an unlikely event. Even though Jasmine has improved and rehabilitated, even if she successfully integrates back into society, she will forever have this as a part of her past. She will also forever have people that look at her as a monster. Her story is known all over the world. Jasmine is the youngest person in Canada to have ever committed such a heinous crime. It is a question to ponder as to whether Jasmine has forgiven herself or if she is forever haunted by the monster that she perhaps did not even know lurked inside her. Perhaps even scarier to think of is the possibility that she really could live without being constantly haunted by the crime. Is there any amount of rehabilitation that should erase that guilt? And then one has to consider Jeremy. Has he come to terms with the events? Is he sorry for his crimes? Will a life in prison in any way begin to repay his debt for those three lives that he so brutally extinguished?

Life in Medicine Hat continues on. It is still a relatively safe place to live. Medicine Hat is still a relatively small tight knit place filled with working class suburbs. There are still nice neighborhoods that feel safe the way that Ross Glen did before tragedy came to town but no one will forget what could happen no matter how nice or normal a family might seem they will know that a tragedy like this could happen to any family because it already has.

KEMBERLY RAMER

There is a shocking truth about which families in the US should be aware. A truth every bit as terrifying as it is essential to know. Around three quarters of a million of American teens and younger children go missing every year. In fact, one child is lost every forty seconds.

As frightening as that figure is, when broken down aspects of it can be put in a more reassuring context. Probably the thing parents fear most is that their child will be abducted, seized by a stranger, perhaps sexually assaulted and murdered. The better news is that of the enormous figures of kids who go missing, only about one hundredth of one per cent are taken by strangers.

That still relates, however, to over one hundred children a year. This means that more than a hundred families, sets of parents and their wider community will be devastated by the horrendous impact caused by the actions of sick, ill, dangerous, criminals over the coming twelve months.

Nevertheless, far more children run away than are taken by strangers, to be discovered later often with their tails between their legs. A further significant number are taken by a family member, often the result of a custody dispute. Or maybe the prospect of such a stressful hearing leads parents to take the law into their own hands. Such action causes enormous heartache – but it can also be understood. Our children are the most important part of our lives; the thought of losing them can cause anyone to act irrationally and behave completely different to normal.

Children get lost when they hurt themselves and cannot get home, or are helped by well meaning strangers. More appear to be lost when a miscommunication is all that has happened. Nevertheless, as great a relief as one of the above brings when it comes to light, the impact on police time and the long term scarring to parents and children alike cannot be underestimated.

The reassuring news for parents is that of the unbelievably high number of kids that do go missing, well over 99% are found safe and well. Not that such an outcome eases the unimaginable fear that comes from discovering a child is missing. Nor does it offer any relief for the tiny percentage of parents who never recover their kids, or are greeted by the terrifying sound of sad faced police officers knocking on their door to deliver the worst possible news.

As parents, our primary function is to protect our offspring. We hold that drive biologically, morally and socially. When we fail, even though the fault does not lie with us, our guilt will never flow away.

In fact, despite the frighteningly high numbers, the amount of kids going missing is actually falling. There are many reasons for that – perhaps most important among them is that cell phones are more and more widespread. That makes communication so much easier, although parents of teens will know that sinking feeling of their child's failure to answer their phone. At least, not until they are ready to do so.

Sex offenders are also better tracked, treated and prevented from engaging in criminal pursuits.

Of course, many of us will counter this with the argument that the internet has opened up new ways for those with wicked intents to get access to our kids. The truth is probably opposite. While there are certainly more than enough cases of online grooming, it is just that. Online. The risk of a vulnerable child going to a groomer's home, or travelling away with them, is much less. They can share their contacts online, the trouble of getting to their so-called friend's home is something they do not need to do. The thought of our child being groomed is, of course, horrendous; but it is better than he or she being abducted.

The growth of the internet has also led an increase in the teaching of safety awareness to young people.

The sad and troubling fact is that when a child does go missing for nefarious reasons, the person who takes them is most often somebody they know.

Given all of the above, something that is a complete rarity occurs when a teenager does go missing, but the authorities have not the slightest indication as to what has happened to them. Even when the news will be the worst imaginable, usually police will have clues or tip offs which lead them hopefully to the living child, but at other times to their body.

So it was unusual in that extreme that in the case of Kemberly Ramer no such information has ever made its way to the authorities. Not to local police, state police, nor the FBI who are also involved in the investigation into what is now accepted to be her abduction.

Kemberly was just seventeen years old when she was last seen. It was August 16th 1997, and the sun was beating mercilessly from the Alabama skies. Kemberly – Kem to her family and friends – was a happy and settled girl. Neither her mother nor her father, who died in 2010, can entertain the thought that she was a runaway. At the time in question, Kem was staying with her father – her parents were divorced. She was enjoying a pleasant summer's day. She had been to a softball game with a group of friends, then travelled with her boyfriend to his house.

She headed home at around 11.00pm – perhaps as late as 11.45pm. But it was only a five minute drive from her boyfriend's house to that of her father. The evidence police later found certainly suggested that she made it back safely.

Then, the next morning, her father went to her room to welcome her to the new day, and found that his daughter was gone. There was some evidence of a struggle, but nothing major. The sheets on her bed were ruffled. There was no suggestion of a forced entry to the house, however. The indications were that Kem had either left of her own accord, or had been forcibly extracted from the house without much of a fight. However, she was a fit girl, 130lbs and 5' 4" tall and in good condition. She could have put up strong resistance if she had wanted to, and there was no evidence of more than a minor struggle. Possibly not even that.

But if she did go out of her own accord, it seems certain that Kem did so with no plans to leave the house. All of her shoes were in situ; she did not put in her contact lenses, and her vision was extremely limited without them. Her purse, car keys and jewellery were intact, although a couple of pieces were missing. These, it seemed to investigators, were items she was already wearing. Her car rested peacefully on the drive.

For her mother, Sue Infinger, Kem's disappearance was understandably perplexing, but she also had clarity about certain aspects of it.

'I don't know why anyone would want to hurt her,' she said. 'I believe it was someone she knew.' Later she stressed the unlikelihood that Kem would have vanished of her own accord. 'She was a great daughter. She was so happy,' she confirmed.

And that, unfortunately, was that. More than twenty years later, neither her family nor the various investigators linked to the case are any closer to finding out what happened in the early hours of that high summer morning.

Kem lived in Opp, a small city in Alabama close to the border with Florida. Alabama is one of the poorer states in the US. When it comes to per capita income, only Mississippi and West Virginia are below it. The five richest states all have average figures 50% above its per head income. Opp matches the pattern of the state, with one in five of its slightly under 7000 population on or below the poverty line.

In fact, Opp is an innocuous little city. Its biggest annual attraction is its Rattlesnake Rodeo, the thought of which brings all kinds of dangerous images to mind. So when one of the popular, intelligent and reliable members of the little community went missing, people did all they could to help out.

Many engaged in on foot searches, others took their 4 x 4 vehicles and pick-up trucks to head off road to search the scrubby, marshy lands that surround the city.

Because Kem really was a well and widely loved young person. She was about to start her senior year in High School when whatever tragedy to befall her struck. Dark haired with distinctive, bushy eyebrows, Kem's all American girl image was emphasised by the clear braces she was still wearing. Kem might have been seventeen, able to drive her own car, but she really remained just a child. On the night she went missing she may have been wearing a white t shirt which was decorated with a brightly coloured design on its front. It had the words 'New Orleans' written under the design. She appeared, judging from which clothes were left behind and which were not, to be wearing cut off grey sweatpants. She had a little jewellery on her person as well. Her gold bracelet and necklace, and an ankle bracelet – also in the style of a gold chain – have never been found.

But whether wearing such casual clothes, or in her softball outfit, or cheerleader uniform, she was a girl with so much ahead of her. Her plans for her future were already well developed. It was her intention, on leaving High School, to enrol in the University of South Alabama, where she would major in physical therapy.

Kem's parents reported her missing first thing on the morning of August 17th 1997. They had spent the previous day calling her friends, speaking to people who knew her and waiting for the smiling face to come through one of their doors. But when that did not happen, they took the difficult step of approaching the police. Doing so marked a point of no return. No longer could they pretend that she was out enjoying herself somewhere, just acting as a forgetful teen who didn't tell her mom and dad where she was going.

Not that this was ever much of a possibility. Kem was not that kind of girl. Quite soon, it became apparent to police that they were looking at an abduction of some kind. With the state line so close, and the prospect that she had been taken into nearby Florida, it became a multi-organisation investigation, and the FBI missing persons unit were called in.

With any case such as this, those closest to home are the first to be investigated. That included her mom, her sister, her dad and her boyfriend. But there was not the slightest shred of evidence linking any of these to her disappearance. All were completely innocent of any criminal action.

But equally, the lack of any kind of serious struggle, the absence of any theft of her property, and with no forensic evidence at her father's home, or in her room, the suggestion was that her abductor was someone she knew. Perhaps she had gotten up to answer a knock on the door late at night, not bothering with shoes or her contact lenses. Perhaps she had welcomed somebody in, only for it to turn unpleasant in her room. But if so, not that unpleasant. There was no signs of a major fight, no blood, no upturned furniture.

Perhaps, instead, it was a stranger – maybe one who entered through a window left ajar, and one who was armed and so able to subdue the young girl. Perhaps even she had woken to think it was her father in her room. He was out the night in question, but maybe she believed he had arrived home early, or was ringing the door bell having forgotten his keys.

The problem for the FBI and the police investigation team was that they had nothing on which to base their investigations. However, sometimes the authorities can be criticised for not acting quickly enough in the case of a missing teenager. In this case, no such charge can be applied. The authorities quickly got to work, and have never stopped trying.

Their first action was to establish that Kem may well have crossed state lines. Donald Clark was a captain with the Walton County Sheriff's Office. He recalled the incident. 'We know she went missing from Opp, Alabama. But the FBI and many different agencies are still involved,' he said.

The various teams quickly got to work. And they did not stop. Searches continued for years. At one point, the FBI employed an infrared plane in the hope that this would penetrate some of the deep wooded land surrounding Opp and spot something that could offer a hint as to what had happened to the seventeen year old. As for family and friends, they would head out every weekend to search firstly this area, and then the next. But no progress was made. Not a hint of a step forward.

'There were all kinds of search efforts. You know, with four wheelers, on foot, and the searches went of for several years,' recalls Kem's mother, Sue. 'Every single weekend we would go out and search.'

But then, in March of the following year, a tip off made its way to the investigating team. It seemed as though Kem's body could be hidden in a well near Coffee County, which is also in Alabama. The authorities took the tip seriously. They brought in a large bulldozer and crashed through the well. A number of cadaver dogs were let loose to see what they could find. In all, this particular search lasted for eight hours. But nothing was found.

This tip off was the first of several moments of hope which Kem's family would experience in the twenty plus years since she disappeared. But each time, that hope has been followed by disappointment. Sue Infinger remains tragically bemused by the whole situation. She has never gained the slightest idea of who might want to hurt her daughter.

Just a couple of months later, an even more reliable indication was received regarding Kem's possible whereabouts. With ironic sadness, the search that followed came on the day of her eighteenth birthday, around nine months after she went missing. That the authorities received not just one but two tip offs which suggested her body could be in a remote, rural lake in Walton County encouraged mis-placed confidence.

Investigators sent a team of eight divers and spent three days searching the pond. In particular, the tips suggested that maybe her missing jewellery might be discovered there. Lighting equipment was employed to try to aid the search of the dark and dank lake. Acid formed there, the result of vegetation. This caused a dark, ink like substance to spread, rendering visibility in the lake to zero. But still the teams searched. However, their failure to discover anything might have been down to conditions that made their search as close to impossible as could be imagined. Equally, they may have found nothing because nothing was there.

At this time, the authorities were receiving regular information about Kem's disappearance. Following the start of the search, several tips came into the local FBI office. Mostly, these related to southern Alabama and the north western corner of Florida. Meanwhile, the FBI was offering a reward of $20000 for any information which might lead to Kem's body, or her remains, being found.

Perhaps it was the money, and the new publicity surrounding the search, that prompted these tips.

By this stage, for Sue and her family, the sad understanding had sunk in that now the search was not for a living, breathing, life enhancing daughter, but for her body. It was a deeply difficult and depressing step to have to take. 'I can't see anybody keeping her hidden for this amount of time without hearing from her. Somebody has done something bad to her. I just feel it,' she said.

However, a steady trickle of calls were making their way to the Holmes County Sheriff's Department. This offered a modicum of hope. 'I know they didn't find anything, but I believe the calls...were just the beginning of this,' she continued. 'I think it's going to open some new doors. I think some people know something. There's still the reward, and sometimes money makes people talk. I just want to find her, and I need people in this area to help find her.'

Unfortunately, that did not prove to be the case.

The case seemed to grow cold following the failed search of the lake. But then, in 2001, an agency in Texas received some kind of indication to search Baptism Hole, a renowned sink hole in the region. This not for profit group took cadaver dogs to the location, and there were several indications from the animals that the hole could be worth searching.

In the end, an ancient engine block was dug up. Significantly, an old rope was attached to it. Could the rope have been tied around a person's body? Might the engine block have been used to weight down that body, so that it stayed firmly out of sight? The not for profit group passed on their findings to the FBI, who arrived the next day to investigate further.

However, once more that spark of hope for Kem's family was extinguished. The FBI's own cadaver dogs found nothing, and the search was called off. Once more, all went quiet on the official front. Meanwhile, in the background Sue continued to keep her daughter's case alive. She knew that only by ensuring the disappearance stayed in the fore front of people's thinking could the chance of a find be maintained. Posters, searches, interviews; along with Kem's sister and other family members, she did everything that she could.

It seemed like this perseverance eventually paid off. In September 2006, more than nine years after Kem had last been seen, the search took a sudden change of direction. Ponce De Leon is a tiny town, some way over the state line in Holmes County, Florida. The region is geographically everything that might be expected from that part of the United States. Heavy greenery shelters swamps and waterways. If somebody wanted to hide a body, and ensure that it would never be found, then it is hard to think of a more suitable location.

A tip came in to police in Opp, indicating that Kem's body could have been hidden there. The authorities believed that tip to be credible, and informed the FBI. Once more, a tiny flicker of hope that something positive might be about to be delivered entered Sue Infinger's consciousness.

The tip off indicated that another sink hole could hold important evidence. This time, the feature sat in private property close to Ponce De Leon, and not far from the busy Route 90. Again, the authorities come out with credit. Nine years after the event, it would have been easy to just pay lip service to this latest tip off, especially given the difficulties searching such a location would present. Instead, the FBI brought in additional cadaver dogs from Baltimore, Maryland. Its divers scoured every possible corner, every passageway, of the sink hole.

For a couple of days, no news was good news. Nothing was making its way to public ears, and that gave the hope that in fact something had been found. Maybe the case of Kemberly Ramer could now move on to its next phase, raising clues towards the identification of her killer and a search for this person. Yet, those hopes were dashed once more. The dogs found no traces, and the divers found nothing. Another dead end, it seemed, had been explored and then abandoned.

Other moments came and went. Interest was aroused when police began to dig in a region fifty miles from Opp. Family and friends headed to watch, and to hope. In fact, the police dig was as a result of a tip off into a completely different search for another missing woman.

'I hate it, but this investigation has nothing to do with Kem,' stated a local Opp police investigator at the time.

However, even though the connection was tenuous in the extreme, there was a small chance that this dig could be connected with the abduction of Kem. Police were actually investigating the disappearance of a woman identified only as 'Ray', who had vanished from the grounds of a motel in 1992. The site was within thirty yards of the discovery of the remains of another woman, Donna Callahan. Although her remains were not found until 1996, she had gone missing from her place of work seven years earlier.

Callahan's killers were eventually found. Mark Riebe along with his half brother William Alex Wells were convicted of the homicide, and Riebe had also long been suspected in the Ray case. Her body has never been found, Callahan's only after a tip off from another prison inmate. That part of the county is poor, full of litter and dirt tracks. Single storey homes are little more than shacks. The south has some areas of astonishing depravation for a country as rich as the US. Is there a possibility that Riebe was also responsible for Ray's killing? And if so, who is to say that this man has not spread his evil even wider? Maybe there are other bodies of young women lying hidden underground somewhere in the region. If they exist, could one of these belong to a young all American girl, a seventeen year old from Opp, Alabama?

One final mystery surrounds Kem's case. A few years after her disappearance, a Walton County deputy was fired from his job. The exact details are hazy, not least because official accounts have remained private.

For Robert Williams, though, the reason for the termination of his contract is clear. It is because he became involved in the investigation into Kem's disappearance. Williams was an officer with a string of commendations behind him, a thirteen year veteran with the Honolulu Police Department. After all other leads appeared to be going nowhere, Williams started his own investigations. Within a short time, he received his first reprimand. Wrapped in legal speak was the clear message to mind his own business and stay out of the investigation.

But Williams was used to working on his own initiative. Perhaps they did things differently in Hawaii. He continued his enquiries, and within a short time another reprimand followed. This time, along with a letter of termination. Local police insist that Williams' case is just based on sour grapes, the political fall out of an election campaign. But the matter has never been properly explained.

But as for official leads and tips, over the last decade they have dried up. Something new will be needed to bring any kind of peace to Sue and her family.

Even today, nearly twenty two years after Kem disappeared, her case remains open, and active. Douglas Astralaga is Chief Division Counsel of the FBI based in Mobile, Alabama. 'Our agents work very closely with every one of the departments and follow up on any leads that come to light,' he said recently. 'We will bring whatever resources are necessary to this investigation.'

Meanwhile, Donald Clark echoes the comments of his FBI colleague. 'I hope we can get her mother some kind of answer of what happened to her (Kem). We ultimately hope to recover her, or the remains of her body,' he said. 'We hope to prosecute whoever did this.'

And those determined comments offer a small crumb of comfort and hope to Kem's family. Perhaps, somewhere, her father too is watching out.

While she could never come to terms with the loss of her daughter, Sue is able to put her indescribable situation into some kind of perspective. Although that perspective is one tragic in the extreme. 'If I could tell her something today,' she says, 'I would tell her I love her very much. And we wish that this has never happened. We all love her, and we aren't giving up until she gets justice.'

It seems, though, that justice will be long in arriving. It may never be reached. Of course, Sue and her family accept now that Kem must be dead. It's just that, tingling away at the furthest corner of the heart and mind remains that faint hope that maybe she isn't. Miracles do happen. People are found. But that tingle hurts; and Sue has no idea whether, even if Kem's remains are one day discovered, if her abductor is brought to justice, it will ever go away.

CLEVELAND TORSO MURDERS

26

NAOMI JAMES

Cleveland has been considered one of the most dangerous cities in the US for some time. In 2008, according to the Morgan Quitno Press National crime rankings, Cleveland was named the 7th most dangerous city in the US; in recent years, the city has seen multiple shootings and homicides as well as many burglaries and robberies.

This is nothing new as Cleveland has had a long history of violence. Kingsbury Run, a piece of land in southeast Cleveland was the infamous site where the Cleveland Torso Murder chose to dump his victims' bodies from the 1930s onwards.

The Cleveland Torso Murder also known as 'The Mad Butcher of Kingsbury Run' was a still unidentified serial killer who got his name for the state of his victims' bodies when they were discovered; they had been beheaded and dismembered at various joints. Officially, the Cleveland Torso Murderer is believed to have killed 12 people, although most guess that this count was much higher.

The Lady Of the Lake

In the late summer of 1934, handyman Joseph Hejduk discovered a broken rib cage and spinal column in the sand on the shores of Lake Erie. Suspecting that they may be human remains, he alerted Country Deputy Sheriff Melvin Keener, who after taking a look at the bones himself, concluded that they were animal bones and instructed Hejduk to bury them in the sand.

On September 5th, two weeks later, and 30 miles away from where Hejduk buried the bones, Photostat operator Frank La Gassie was carrying out his morning routine of scouring the beaches of Lake Erie for driftwood. While beach-combing, La Gssie noticed a strange object sticking out of the sand. After examining it at close range, he was horrified to discover that it was the lower half of a woman's torso, amputated above the knees. La Gossie immediately alerted the authorities, who speculated that the woman may have committed suicide, after which her body was torn apart by the propeller of a boat.

However, when the torso arrived at the Coroner's office, Coroner Arthur Pearce ruled out the suicide angle. After examining the body, he deduced that while the body had been in the lake for four months, the woman had been dead for six. The cuts which had dismembered her torso were precise and clean; done with a practiced human hand as opposed to the random motion of a boat propeller. And, the body's flesh was tough, red and leathery - evidence that it had been exposed to a chemical solution, which examiners later decided must have been calcium hypochloride or chloride of lime.

After the press caught wind of the discovery and published the sensational news reports about it, Hejduk came forward to show the police the area where he had buried the bones. After recovering and testing the bones, investigators concluded that they too had belonged to the woman, who by this time was being called the 'Lady of The Lake'.

Authorities then began scouring the shores of Lake Erie, which is over 25 square kilometers large.

Despite the search and the reports, the authorities were only able to find one other body part of the Lady of the Lake; the upper part of an arm. This scattering of body parts left the investigators with no means of identifying the Lady of the Lake. Without an identification or any other clues about why the woman had been murdered, the case quickly went cold. Just over a week after the torso was found, the woman's remains were placed in a box and buried in the Highland Park Cemetery.

In the coming years, many similarities between the Lady of the Lake case and the yet-to-be-discovered victims of the Torso Murderer would be evident. For one, the victims were all dismembered with precision; the murderer clearly knew his way around the human body. Many of the victims would have died from decapitation and many would remain unidentified. Their body parts were scattered across Kingsbury Run and its water bodies; many parts would never be recovered.

At that time, however, the police and press treated the Lady of the Lake as a one-off, sensational case. They had no idea that this was the work of a serial killer and that two years later, the Lady of the Lake would be renamed victim#0 and acknowledged as one of the first known victims of the Cleveland Torso murderer.

Edward Andrassy and The Unidentified Victim

A year after the Lady of the Lake was discovered, in September 1935, two teenage boys; James Wagner and Peter Kostura were playing ball in Kingsbury Run. At the time, Kingsbury Run was home to a collection of dilapidated homes, inhabited by some of the poorest people in Cleveland; it was often referred to as a "hobo jungle".

While chasing their ball at the bottom of Jackass Hill, Wagner and Kostura came across the corpse of a headless, emasculated man, naked, except for a pair of socks. A little while after the terrified boys reported their find, detectives arrived at the scene and found the headless corpse's severed genitals and, disturbingly, another headless corpse, which was partially decomposed. The heads of both corpses were buried nearby and the detectives also found a few blood-stained clothes, some rope, a torch and bucket containing a little engine oil.

After Coroner Pearce arrived at the scene, he deduced that the decomposed corpse had been the first to die - he estimated that he had been dead ten days, while the second corpse had been dead only a few days; the cause of death for both was decapitation. He also noticed that the little skin which remained on the decomposed skin was red, tough and leathery; similar to what was seen on the Lady of the Lake.

While it was impossible to secure fingerprints from the decomposed corpse, the investigators were able to get fingerprints from the second, emasculated corpse. After a search in the police database, the investigators were able to identify the corpse as the body of Edward Andrassy, a hospital orderly, who had been booked for petty crimes. Police in the area were familiar with Edward W Andrassy as he had the reputation of being a troublemaker and had been arrested in the past for being involved in brawls, having drunk too much and for carrying a concealed weapon on one occasion.

In 'In The Wake of the Butcher', an extensively researched nonfiction account of the Torso murder, James Jessen Badal, a Cleveland writer and teacher writes, "Though hardly a major criminal, Andrassy was well known to the police as something of a gadfly, a perpetual source of trouble, a constant thorn in the side of law enforcement. He frequently haunted the sleazy establishments of Rowdy Row... He shot craps with his friends and supposedly even slept off some of his drunks in a graveyard."

Andrassy had been married and had a daughter; however, some suggested he may have been homosexual. Indeed, after his body was identified, the press delved deep into Andrassy's unstable life, highlighting his scuffles with the law, his unemployment, and his deviant behavior.

On their part, the police also believed that Andrassy's murder could have been related to his lifestyle. They looked into all his acquaintances, many of whom also frequented the Roaring Third, a collection of brothels, saloons, and pawn houses. During their investigation, they learned that he had possibly acted as a pimp for girls he knew and had also possibly stabbed an Italian during a bar brawl. They also found acquaintances who revealed that Andrassy had had sexual relations with several men and they claimed he had been having an affair with a married woman; some said that her husband had found out and had threatened to kill Andrassy.

Speculations ran rife among the police force about why Andrassy may have been killed. In

Torso: The Story of Eliot Ness and the Search for a Psychopathic Killer', Steven Nickel, the author of the 1989 book, chronicles some of these: "Detective Sergeant Bernard Wolf, Head of the Homicide Unit, maintained that the double murder was the result of a perverted love triangle. A number of his men agreed since the emasculation of the bodies suggested sexual slayings... A few pointed out that it was not uncommon when the body left behind in a Mafia killing had its genitals mutilated." The investigators agreed that the second victim; the unidentified older man was an acquaintance of Andrassy, and that both had been involved in a shady matter which led to their deaths possibly a love triangle gone awry.

Ultimately, however, all the cops' speculations panned out to nothing; all their leads dissolved upon further investigation. Andrassy's body was buried at the St Mary's Cemetery, while the unidentified victim was buried in Potter's Field.

The Body in the Bushel Basket

Less than six months later, in January 1936, a woman saw a dog sniffing around two halves of a bushel basket which had been left outside the Hart Manufacturing building on Central Avenue near East 20th Street in Cleveland. After taking a closer look, she decided it was a basket of hams. However, a little while later, butcher Charles Paige placed a frantic call to the police; someone had recognized that the basket did not contain 'hams', but pieces of a body. Once they arrived, the police opened the baskets to find half of a headless torso wrapped in newspaper.

The body was taken in for an autopsy and Coroner Pearce found that the woman had been dead for at least two days and the cause of death was decapitation. However, her body had been dismembered after death. A few weeks later, the rest of the victim's body was discovered in a vacant lot.

Using fingerprints from the body, investigators were able to identify the victim as Florence Genevieve Pollilo who lived on the edge of the Roaring Third Street, considered the red light district of Cleveland. Like Andrassy, Polillo had a disreputable lifestyle. She was a 41-year-old prostitute, notorious in the area.

She was born in 1891 as Florence Genevieve Sawdy to a laborer father and homemaker mother. The family was perpetually on the move, possibly to go wherever Polillo's father found work and therefore records of her early days are few and far between.

As an adult, Polillo was arrested multiple times for solicitation and selling liquor; indeed, just a few months before her body was discovered in October 1935, she was arrested for selling alcohol. However, despite having a record of several of Polillo's misdemeanors and contacting her acquaintances, the police were no closer to finding out who had killed her. And, despite similarities to the Kingsbury Run victims, they shied away from making a connection. Nickel writes "'Detective Sergeant James T Hogan, the newly appointed Head of Homicide, refused to acknowledge a parallel to the four-month-old murders of Andrassy and his unknowns companion, despite the unusual feature of death by decapitation."

The Tattooed Man, and More Victims

However, when the next victim was found in June 1936, it was harder not to acknowledge a connection. One morning, while playing in Kingsbury Run near the East 55th Street Bridge, two boys found the head of a male wrapped in a pair of trousers. A day later the police found the victim's body; it had been drained of blood and had six tattoos. Again, the coroner ruled that the cause of death was decapitation. Despite securing fingerprints from the body, the 'tattooed man', as he was nicknamed by the press was never identified. A plaster model of the man's head and a chart displaying the description and location of the tattoos were displayed at the Great Lakes Exposition of 1986. Over 100,000 people are reported to have seen this representation, but none came forward to identify him.

A month later in July, while hiking in the woods near Clinton Road, near Big Creek, Marie Barkley discovered a headless body. This victim, the Coroner estimated, had been dead for around two months. Again, the cause of death was decapitation, but unlike the other victims, it appeared that this victim had been killed at the same spot the body was found; large amounts of blood had been absorbed by the land.

By this time, the media, as well as several police officers who had been involved in the case, had begun suspect that the increasing body count was, in fact, the work of a serial killer. In 'In the Wake of the Butcher', Badal comments "Sergeant James T Hogan was deeply apprehensive. Although the chief of homicide had not been among those at the foot of Jackass Hill when the bodies of Edward Andrassy and his unnamed companion were discovered year before, he had been one of the first behind Hart Manufacturing the following January to investigate the death of Flo Polillo...He had responded to the call when...found the head of the tattooed man in Kingsbury Run on June 5, 1936 and had been among the first on the scene when the body was discovered the next day. Up until early June 1936, he had regarded the killings as separate crimes, but the murder of the still unidentified tattooed man forced him to reassess his position and see them as linked."

This hunch was cemented when in September 1936, twenty-five- year -old Jerry Harris spotted two halves of a male torso floating in a creek in Kingsbury Run. After the police, including ding Sergeant Hogan, arrived on the scene, they fished out two halves of a headless, legless armless torso which had belonged to a white male. His head was never recovered, although his lower torso and parts of both legs were later found.

After noting several similarities to the earlier crimes - the decapitated body and pieces of clothing nearby - Sergeant Hogan told the press that the man had been killed by the same person who had murdered Andrassy, Polillo, The Tattooed Man and the two unidentified victims. The police had confirmed that a serial killer was on the loose.

When talking to the press, Coroner Pierce highlighted the killer's knowledge of the human anatomy, explaining how the cuts on the body were clean and precise. "Judging from the character of the cut through the bone, it would require either a gore with a heavier knife or some heavier instrument as a hatchet or cleaver to do this," Pierce said.

On September 11th, Cleveland News published a piece on what was 'known' about the killer. "The killer is apparently a sex maniac of the sadistic type. This is indicated by the condition of his victims. He is probably a muscular man. The killer definitely has expert knowledge of human anatomy. The incisions of his knife are clean and were made in each case without guesswork. He may have gathered his knowledge of anatomy as a medical student or it is possible that he is a butcher." The Cleveland Press and The Cleveland Plain Dealer also devoted considerable print space to the killer and his victims.

In the press, a report described the killer saying "He kills for the thrill of killing. He kills to satisfy a bestial, sadistic lust for blood. He kills to prove himself strong. He kills to feed his sex-perverted brain the sight of a beheaded human. He must kill."

This rhetoric, of an unknown, sadistic fiend became common in the news. The stories about the Torso murderer had been picked up by national and even international news; the world's attention was on Cleveland. He had become notorious as 'The Mad Butcher of Kingsbury Run'.

A Dedicated Task Force

By this time, the Cleveland public and indeed America as a whole was understandably uneasy. However, there was one beacon of hope; Eliot Ness.

Ness was well-known at the time for having investigated and raided several of gangster Al Capone's illegal breweries and supply routes. He assembled a team of 11 men, who were nicknamed 'The Untouchables' for their commitment to their cause and the law. In 1934, he was promoted to the Chief Investigator of the Prohibition Bureau for Chicago and in 1935, Cleveland's mayor, Harold Burton appointed him as Cleveland's Safety Director.

During the first year of his appointment, Ness was somewhat removed from the investigations into the torso murders. In his book, Eliot Ness: The Rise and Fall of an American Hero, Douglas Perry attempts to explain why: "... he recognized the killings as the work of a psychopath. Such crimes defied logic. They required luck to solve, and Eliot didn't like to rely on luck. He also didn't like to delve into the dark recesses of men's motivations."

However, after the Tattooed Man was discovered, Mayor Burton summoned Eliot and instructed him to take an active role in the investigations. So, on September 12th, Ness officially began work on the case. After reviewing the case, by interviewing officers involved, he assigned officers to patrol Kingsbury Run, to question its inhabitants and pull out all stops to unearth any shred of evidence about the killer's identity.

At the same time, the Police Chief, Matowitz assigned Peter Merylo and Martin Zalewski on a full-time basis to the case. Merylo reviewed the history to construct a profile of the killer saying "I am of the opinion that the murderer is a sex degenerate, suffering from necrophilia, aphrodisia or erotomania."

This man would not stop killing as long as he is at large and alive," Merylo is reported to have said.

The two detectives also scoured Kingsbury Run, interviewing residents, trailing vague suspects like doctors and butchers and even going undercover as hobos to see if they could find any leads.

More Victims

Despite the multiple investigators' efforts, they could find no substantial lead about who the killer might be. For a couple of months, all was quiet.

However, come February 1937, another victim was discovered; a man found the upper half of a woman's torso near Brahtenahl, a village near Cleveland. By this time, Coroner Pierce had been replaced by Coroner Sam Gerber, who stated that the woman was in her mid-thirties and that the now familiar decapitation had happened after the woman had died. Because of a lack of material to follow up, the woman was never identified.

Then, in June 1837 a young boy found a skull under the Lorain-Carnegie bridge with a burlap bag next to it, which held a skeleton. After analyzing it, Gerber reported that the skeleton had belonged to a petite black woman. Dental records helped detectives identify the victim, as Rose Wallace who, like earlier victim Polillo, had been linked with prostitution.

A month later, another body was discovered by a guardsman in the Cuahoga River. The body, which had belonged to a male in his mid to late thirties had been gutted and its heart had been ripped out. This victim was never identified.

Dr. Francis Sweeny as a Suspect

In March 1938, a severed human leg was discovered. However, this was in Ohio's Sandusky town, some sixty miles away from Cleveland. Nevertheless, investigators from Cleveland took an interest when the Sandusky coroner commented that the leg had been amputated cleanly. After inspecting the leg, David Cowles, the police department's Superintendent of Criminal Identification confirmed that it may have been the work of the Torso Murderer and directed Ness' attention to Dr. Francis Sweeny.

Dr. Sweeney was a World War veteran who checked himself in and out of the Veteran's hospital near Sandusky. He had been brought to Cowles' attention by contacts at the nearby Osborn State Prison Penitentiary Honor Farm, and was of interest because of reported mental imbalances and an old psychiatric evaluation that stated he "had a frustrated desire to operate."

While Ness' team was observing Dr. Sweeney, parts of a body were discovered, yet again in the Cuyahoga River. A laborer spotted half of a woman's leg floating in the water and the police later recovered two burlap bags from the river. They contained more parts of the legs and the woman's torso. Interestingly, Coroner Gerber found drugs in the victim's system and stated that the victim had been killed only a few days before the body's discovery.

While the victim would not be identified, one important outcome of this latest count is that Ness decided to 'arrest' Dr. Sweeney. They picked him up on a street corner and locked him in a room in the Cleveland Hotel. They began to interrogate him, sometimes using brutality. However, Dr. Sweeney failed to give them a clear answer to many of their questions - while he didn't admit to the crimes, he didn't deny them either, choosing only to answer in taunts and riddles.

The investigators also made Dr. Sweeny take two lie detector tests, both of which he failed. However, lie detector tests were not considered irrefutable evidence and would therefore not stand in court. With no other hard evidence and no confession, Eliot Ness was forced to let Dr. Sweeney go.

Taunting Eliot Ness

Ness had lost the case's one somewhat substantial suspect. Then, adding grievous insult to injury on August 16th, 1938, scrap collectors sifting through a dump at East 9th and Lakeside found a woman's torso wrapped in a quilt and man's blazer. Her head, legs, and arms were found nearby in a box wrapped in brown paper. A little way away, the police discovered parts of a second body.

Both the bodies had been dumped in a location that was clearly visible from Ness' office; it seemed as if the killer was taunting him.

In response, two days later, Ness and a team of thirty-five raided the tenements in Kingsbury Run, first evacuating it and then searching the makeshift homes for clues. After a thorough search, the huts and homes were set on fire. "Burn it to the ground," Ness is reported to have said to the fire chief.

This extreme action was met with criticism from the media; an editorial in the Press following the raid said "The throwing into jail of men broken by experience and the burning of their wretched places of habitation will not solve the economic problem. Nor is it likely to lead to the solution of the most macabre mystery in Cleveland's history."

Indeed, the raid had not helped the police recover clues as to the identity of the killer. However, following the raid, there were two developments. Dr. Sweeney checked himself into a mental institution. And, there were to be no more discoveries of victims and it appeared that the murders had stopped.

Frank Dolezal's Arrest

However, even though the murders had stopped, there were still several loose ends; the major one being that the serial killer had still not been conclusively identified. In August 1939, Sheriff Martin O'Donnell arrested Frank Dolezal a Cleveland resident who had lived with Flo Polillo and had possibly been acquainted with Rose Wallace and Edward Andrassy. At this point, Sheriff O'Donnell's son had married Congressman, Martin Sweeney's daughter. Frank Sweeney was Martin Sweeney's cousin.

At one point, Dolezal did confess to murdering Polillo, but later recanted his confession, saying he had been beaten and forced into it. Dolezal was found hanging in his cell in the Cuyahoga County jail with several injured ribs.

Till date, few researchers believe that Dolezal could have been behind the murders.

A Message From The Murderer?

Many who had been involved in the case believed that the murderer was still at large, active and had possibly just shifted to another location. Perry writes, "Detective Merylo, however, had reached the conclusion that the case was much bigger than Cleveland, that the murderer rode the rails and used boxcars as a traveling 'murder laboratory...''

Six months after the discovery of the last victim, someone claiming to be the murderer sent the Cleveland Police Chief George J.Matowitz a letter which was postmarked from Los Angeles. It said "You can rest easy now as I have moved out to sunny California for the winter. I feel bad operating on those people, but science must advance...They called me mad and a butcher, but 'the 'truth will out'.

James Badal's Theory

However, according to James Badal, the murderer could not have been in California because he was Ness' original suspect; Dr. Sweeney. In an interview with Cleveland Magazine he tells the story of Emil Fronek:

" In November 1934, Fronek supposedly was walking up Broadway Avenue, looking for food. He said he found himself on the second floor of a doctor's office. The doctor said, "I'll give you a meal." While Emil was shoveling the food down, he began to feel woozy and wondered if he'd been drugged. So he ran down the steps, onto Broadway, and into Kingsbury Run, got into a boxcar, fell asleep and awoke three days later. He said he went back to Broadway and East 55th, but couldn't find the doctor."

Badal later tells the interviewer that he was approached by a man who claims that his uncle, Edward Peterka, who was a doctor worked with Francis Sweeny. Peterka he said, had set up a medical facility in his house, with the lower floor as a practice and the upper floor as living quarters. He adds that the building had an upper floor, which Sweeney may have been allowed to access.

Badal said "I'm assuming any one of those doctors could've had access to that upper floor, and his colleagues realized he was going through a rough patch. His wife had sued for divorce. If you want to hang out there, go ahead." Nadal says. "He could've very easily gone down to seedy bars closer to the center of town, struck up a relationship and said, "Hey, you want some good booze? Really good stuff? Maybe even drugs?" And then he would take them up these back steps, probably drug them the same way he tried to drug Emil Fronek."

Many familiar with the case agree with Badal's theory. However, till date there's been no ultimate resolution on the identity of the Cleveland Torso Killer and why he was on his killing spree. The ' Mad Butcher of Kingsbury Run's true identity remains shrouded in mystery.

ARTHUR BISHOP

45

DON AINGE

Arthur Gary Bishop—also known as Roger Downs and Lynn Jones—was a child molester/serial killer who sexually abused and murdered five young boys near Salt Lake City, Utah, between 1979 and 1983; at the height of serial killing in the United States. His preferred method of murder was either drowning or beating his helpless victims with a hammer. He was ultimately executed on 9 June 1988 by lethal injection after voluntary waiving any appeal claims.

Early Life

Arthur Gary Bishop was born on 29 September 1952 in Hinckley, Utah, a very small desert town with fewer than 700 residents that lies 100 miles southwest of Salt Lake City in Millard County. The eldest of six brothers, Bishop was raised by his parents as a devout Mormon and excelled in school, earning honor roll status, as well as becoming an Eagle Scout. Despite defense attorneys describing Bishop as a "lonely, frightened child" during his trial, there was no evidence to support said claim. In actuality, he appeared to be a model son and devout Mormon and the specter of abuse never came into public discourse.

School classmates remembered Bishop as "a geek, rarely if ever finding someone who would accept the rare offer of a date." His election as business manager for the high school student council failed to improve his popularity and classmates, again, said that voting a nerd to student council was "a tradition" and "a joke to humble the social elite during the coming year."

Nevertheless, Bishop's younger brother Douglas, four years his junior, idolized his big brother. So much, in fact, that Douglas was arrested and convicted of molesting and sexually assaulting 26 boys between five and 17 years of age from 1976 to 1983 outside of Provo, Utah. He is currently serving four terms of five-years-to-life and, interestingly, the brothers were arrested within three days of each other; however, at the time Douglas did not know where his brother was or what he had done. Despite being diagnosed as a homosexual pedophile himself, Douglas maintained that neither Arthur nor Douglas suffered any sexual abuse as children.

Upon graduating from high school in 1969, Bishop served as a missionary for the Church of Jesus Christ of the Latter Day Saints in the Philippines when he was 19 years of age. Bishop then graduated from Steven-Henager College—a business school that guarantees its students with "fast-track, career specific education"—with honors with a major in accounting and appeared to be following a stable and devout path to success.

However, despite Bishop's seeming normalcy, he possessed a darker side that nobody could have ever guessed by his overt success. He was addicted to and enthralled by child pornography and cultivated and nurtured fantasies which elaborated upon the images with which he was so enamored. It is impossible to ascertain when Bishop crossed that line from his morbid daydreams into becoming an active pedophile; however, experts surmise that a year after his excommunication he finally succumbed to the evil within him.

In February 1978, Bishop was convicted of embezzling nearly $9,000 from a used car dealership where he had been employed as a bookkeeper and, based upon his alleged repentance whether genuine or not, received a five-year suspended sentence on his promise of restitution; however, instead of returning the money he, instead, disappeared. A warrant for his arrest was subsequently issued. His failure to surrender caused the Mormon Church to excommunicate him in October 1978. When Bishop disappeared, he ended all communication with his family and friends, moved to another city, and reemerged as Lynn E. Jones and, later, Roger W. Downs.

By October of that same year he took on the alias of Roger Downs in Salt Lake City proper. He joined the Big Brother program to spend time with disadvantaged youth and his charisma and pseudo-father persona attracted numerous children who he lured into spending time with him at his home or joining him on camping trips; thus potentially providing him victims. At one point, spokespeople for the Big Brother/Big Sister organization admitted receiving tips that a Mr. Downs had molested at least two children while working with them; however, neither of the victims was Bishop's "little brother." Allegedly, police were notified but did nothing with the information.

The Crimes

Alonzo Daniels, 4

The first young boy to disappear was four-year-old Alonzo Daniels, reported missing on 14 October 1979 from his Salt Lake City apartment complex. His worried mother enlisted the help of relatives and friends to search their complex and neighborhood but the young boy was never found. When police started conducting door-to-door searches they first talked to neighbor Roger Downs as his apartment was across the hall from where Daniels and his mother lived. Bishop answered the police's routine questions and denied having any knowledge of the location of the boy. At this point, unbeknownst to the police and his mother the child was already dead.

Bishop had lured Daniels to his home with the promise of candy. He attempted to undress and fondle the young boy in his living room but when the child began to cry and threatened to tell his mother Bishop struck him with a hammer. This did not stop the boy's sobbing so Bishop carried him into the bathroom and drowned him in the tub. When the child was dead Bishop stuffed him into a large cardboard box and took it out to his car; walking right past Daniels' mother who was in the courtyard calling out her son's name.

Over the next few days hundreds of civilians and Salt Lake County's search and rescue team joined the hunt for young Daniels. Among the civilians were faculty and students from the University of Utah and members of a local Teamsters union. Descriptions of the child and descriptions of his clothing were printed and broadcast throughout the entire state. Police had questioned hundreds of people to no avail.

That night Bishop drove the corpse in the box to Cedar Fort, 20 miles southwest of Salt Lake City, and buried the child in the desert with only the trees that gave the nearby town its name as his gravestone.

While driving home, Bishop struggled with myriad emotions: revulsion at what he had done, fear of arrest, perverse excitement, and an overriding belief that he would, in fact, kill again unless he sought some type of help.

Kim Peterson, 11

During the year between Daniels' murder and his next one, Bishop pursued what he believed to be a less dangerous outlet for his uncontrollable and deadly urges. He began to kill puppies he adopted from Salt Lake City animal shelters. Such behavior is one aspect of the well-known triad of characteristics common to serial killers with the other two being bedwetting and setting fires. Over a span of 12 months Bishop adopted as many as 20 homeless puppies, essentially using them as surrogates for children. He later told investigators that "it was so stimulating" and that a puppy's whines were just like Daniels' own cries were. He would get frustrated at the puppies and then bludgeon them with hammers, drown them, or strangle them. It is unknown as to whether Bishop's neighbors knew of his activities; however, at the time, animal cruelty was a simple misdemeanor. Once he grew bored and discovered that the puppies failed to satisfy his urges Bishop went back to molesting children; using lures or threats to prevent them from reporting him.

The next young boy to vanish was 11-year-old Kim Peterson. On 8 November 1980, Peterson had spoken to a man about roller skates at the local skating rink with Kim mentioning that he wanted to sell his pair to purchase another. Bishop told the child he would pay him $35 for his skates. The next day, Peterson left home to go to the rink to sell them. Whereas both of Peterson's parents knew that he had found a buyer, neither of them knew who the mystery man was as no names were mentioned.

As Peterson had promised his parents he would come right home after the sale, when he failed to return they called the police and another fruitless search began. Witnesses at the rink reported that a child matching Peterson's description was talking to a white male, approximately 25 to 35 years of age who weighed around 200 pounds and had a full face, dark hair, and glasses, and clad in blue jeans and am army-style jacket was seen talking to Peterson earlier that day. One witness claimed that the man and the boy had driven away in a silver Chevy Camaro with out-of-state license plates; perhaps from Nevada. However, every lead was useless.

At this time, the police saw no similarity between their suspect and the Roger Downs who lived in an apartment a few blocks from the Petersons' home. Whereas they, again, questioned him routinely, they failed to make a connection between Peterson's disappearance and the disappearance of young Daniels the previous year.

Bishop had bludgeoned Peterson to death with a hammer and buried his body in the desert near where he had buried Daniels' body.

At this point, Bishop realized that murder was far easier the second time and surmised that there was plenty of room in the desert to bury children. While he still feared arrest, he spared his victims if they promised not to talk; however, he was discovering the incomparable rush that murder provided him that was better than any drug.

Danny Davis, 4

On 20 October 1981, four-year-old Danny Davis vanished at a busy supermarket in southern Salt Lake County while shopping with his grandmother. Prior to his kidnapping, Bishop (who later told detectives that while browsing through a local grocery store) "saw the most beautiful little boy kneeling in the aisle" as Davis was trying to get a gumball out of one of the store's machines. Bishop offered Davis some candy but the boy refused. As he was leaving the store Bishop happened to glance behind him to see Davis walking in his direction. He waited for the boy and then led him into the parking lot. Davis' grandmother couldn't find him when she had finished shopping and, as would be expected, panicked. Employees and customers searched the store and parking lot but couldn't find the young boy.

Witnesses said that they remembered a small boy near the gumball machine but could not identify photos of Davis. Others recalled a smiling man talking to Davis but could not give a clear description. They also reported that Davis was seen leaving the store with a man and a woman; however, the woman remains unknown. Witnesses also underwent hypnosis; however, while descriptions of the smiling man were clarified no identification could be made.

Police subsequently launched one of the biggest searches in Utah history trying to find the young boy. Fliers were printed with Davis' photo and copies were sent to law enforcement agencies across the country. A $20,000 reward was offered but nobody had any useful leads. Calls to the Federal Bureau of Investigation (FBI), the National Crime Information Center (NCIC), and Child Find were all to no avail.

Despite hundreds of searchers and the FBI scouring nearby neighborhoods, mountains, lakes, and woods, the young boy was never found. Concern increased as Davis was clad only in blue jeans, a t-shit, and thong sandals when last seen and the temperatures were dropping into the 30's at night. After no luck for two days, divers then searched Big Cottonwood Creek, ponds, roadside ditches, and even went through garbage dumpsters in hundreds of alleys.

At the time, Bishop—still under his alias of Downs—lived a mere half a block from the store and, again, was routinely questioned; however, the police still made no connection that the "same clueless neighbor" had lived in close proximity to all of the missing children. In fact, by the time police visited Bishop in his rented house, Davis was already dead.

Bishop molested the young boy and then silenced his crying by manually pinching his nose and covering his mouth until the child died. The following day Bishop, again, drove to Cedar Fort and buried his third victim beside the other two. Bishop believed that he had a foolproof plan as the Salt Lake City Police Department still had no clue.

After the fact—and much too late—neighbors did mention to police that Mr. Downs had an unusual fondness for children.

Bishop had no need for the reward offer as he still had ample money from his latest embezzlement scheme.

While Bishop was, indeed, cunning and was able to keep the police at bay, state legislators sprang into action as a result of numerous child disappearances. In August 1982, three-year-old Rachel Runyan was kidnapped from a school playground in Sunset; a mere 30 miles north of Salt Lake City. Discovery of her strangled corpse led to numerous calls for action by many organizations and the legislature passed another law.

Whereas first-degree murder was already a capital offense in Utah, the growing indignation with child abductions provided the impetus for the state legislature to add mandatory five-, ten-, or 15-year sentences for convicted child abductors. While this action was all fine and dandy it didn't get investigators any closer to finding out who was responsible for the recent missing children.

Eventually investigators dismissed any possible link between Runyan's murder and the missing Salt Lake City boys. However, there was still much speculation with respect to the disappearances of Daniels, Peterson, and Davis. Detectives from both the Salt Lake and Davis County Sheriff's Departments met with city police departments and FBI agents to try to come up with a lead. Since each of the boys had disappeared at different times of the day and on different days, speculation as to the abductor's employment was frustrated. Investigators also dismissed a clear link between the three boys as most killers tend to prey on members of their own race so while Peterson and Davis were Caucasian, Daniels was African-American. Additionally, Peterson was three times older than both Daniels and Davis. Thus any potential for a pedophile who stalked preschool children was dismissed as well.

By June 1983 almost two years had passed since the last child disappeared. That was to change.

Troy Ward, 6

Bishop's fourth victim was Troy Ward who was abducted on 23 June 1983, his sixth birthday. He was taken from a park near his home where he was permitted to play. Ward was supposed to meet a family friend at 4:00 p.m. at a predetermined street corner and the friend would drive him home to a surprise party. However, when 4:00 came and went with no signs of the child the friend drove to the Ward's residence hoping that the child was, perhaps, already there.

Police were immediately called and officers commenced searching the area around the park. One witness remembered seeing a boy who matched Ward's description leaving the scene with a man on foot just prior to 4:00 p.m. The witness assumed them to be father and son as they looked completely at ease with each other.

Of course, that man was Bishop who had just taken his fourth victim back to his home where—not unlike his other victims—Ward was sexually assaulted, bludgeoned with a hammer, and then drowned in the bathtub. Bishop later stated that he initially thought of letting the boy go; however, Ward's last-minute threats to expose Bishop led to his demise.

Afterward, instead of driving to his own private graveyard near Cedar Fort, Bishop drove east and buried the boy near Big Cottonwood Creek in the Twin Peaks Wilderness Area.

Bishop again realized how easy everything was and he decided not to wait another two years to kill again. He waited less than a month.

Graeme Cunningham, 13

On 14 July, 13-year-old Graeme Cunningham disappeared from his home two days before he was planning on attending a camping trip with a junior high classmate and their chaperone: 32-year-old Roger Downs. The boy was excited for his trip and was already all packed. That Thursday afternoon, two days before he was to leave, Cunningham vanished from his neighborhood without a trace; thus prompting his parents to call the police when he didn't come home for dinner.

The abduction made the news and Bishop visited Cunningham's mother to offer any help he could in finding her son. Police drew similarities to John Wayne Gacy who was convicted of murdering and burying under his house 33 victims and was seen talking with the last of his victims before that victim disappeared. The literature is rife with examples of serial killers who let down their guards and committed clumsy and costly mistakes. They wondered if Mr. Downs had committed a similar mistake by offering his help to his fifth victim's mother.

Investigation and Arrest

Bishop was again questioned. However, this time the police began to dig into his background and discovered his close proximity to all of the young male victims as well as an "almost unnatural fondness for neighborhood children." Sergeant Bruce White and Detective Steven Smith offered an invitation for Bishop to come to the police station to help find Cunningham. Veteran homicide detective Don Bell was waiting on their arrival and slowly and surely Bell began to pick apart Bishop's story.

They also discovered he was wanted under another alias, Lynn Jones, for embezzling $10,000 from an employer by writing bad checks in his boss' name before stealing his own personnel file from the office and vanishing. Police utilized the pending embezzlement charge to arrest Bishop to give them more time to investigate his possible link in the young boys' disappearances.

By sundown that day investigators had gotten Bishop to confess to five murders spanning four years.

The following morning Bishop took authorities to the Cedar Fort area where he pointed out the graves where Daniels', Peterson's, and Davis' remains were recovered. Bishop then led police another 65 miles south to Big Cottonwood Creek where Ward's and Cunningham's more recently deceased bodies were unearthed.

Autopsy results showed signs of sexual abuse on Ward's and Cunningham's remains. The other two had been buried far too long to provide any useful similar forensic evidence.

When Bishop's house was searched police discovered a .38 caliber gun, a bloodstained mallet and hammer, dozens of photographs of one of his victims taken after his abduction, and other pictures of nude boys which were framed to avoid their faces and, therefore, conceal their identities. Investigators also recovered a book entitled *100 Ways to Disappear and Live Free* that suggested that Bishop had studied how to be a fugitive from justice.

Additional investigation revealed that Bishop had molested dozens of other young boys over the years but did not kill them. After public announcement that Bishop was in custody and had confessed, the police were inundated with calls from parents who claimed that Bishop molested their children, or the children of acquaintances. His reasons for sparing their lives were never fully uncovered. Whereas a number of parents allegedly knew about Bishop's "activities" none of them had approached police during the four-year search for a child murderer, likely due to the fact that Bishop was a devout Mormon who tried to help disadvantaged children, or, perhaps, these parents did not want to admit or accept what happened to their children.

Bishop was charged with five counts of capital murder, five counts of kidnapping, two counts of forcible sexual assault, and one count of sexually abusing a minor; the sexual abuse evidence only applicable to his two most recent victims. Of course, murder was the charge that truly mattered in that if the state successfully proved its case Bishop would be sentenced to death.

Trial

Bishop's trial commenced on 27 February 1984 and lasted until 19 March.

Deputy County Attorney Robert Stott described Bishop as a "ruthless killer and sexual deviant possessed of 'a scheming, calculating, cunning mind.'" However, Bishop made his crimes sound awfully simple. He had said that one can offer children anything and they would go with complete strangers.

Bishop's defense team was led by Jo Carol Nesset-Sale who had very little realistic hope of getting their client acquitted as his confession alone had guaranteed that he would spend, at least, the rest of his life in prison. Therefore, his attorneys tried to mitigate Bishop's crimes in the hope of replacing first-degree murder charges with manslaughter. They argued that Bishop's emotional and psychological "deficits" drove him to kill and that "for some reason [he was] stuck or fixated with a sexual attraction to little boys. He never outgrew these erotic feelings. He was a lonely, frightened child." These words were later quoted by author Clifford L. Linedecker in his 1990 book *Serial Thrill Killers*.

His attorneys claimed that one of the primary culprits behind Bishop's fixation and deviance was pornography. Dr. Victor Cline was called as an expert witness and testified pornography had warped Bishop's mind to the extent that he was rendered unable to resist his attraction to children or to the murderous urges that followed. Bishop later stated in an interview with the *Salt Lake Tribune* that Dr. Cline's testimony made him realize what he was. He said:

"During my trial ... Dr. Victor Cline testified about the adverse effects of pornography. As I listened to his explanations, I could discern how my own life desires escalated. These normal feelings become desensitized, and they tend to act out what they have seen. So it was with me. I am a homosexual pedophile convicted of murder, and pornography was a

determining factor in my downfall. Somehow I became sexually attracted to young boys, and I would fantasize about them naked...I would need pictures that were more explicit and shortly the images became commonplace and acceptable. Finding and procuring sexually arousing materials became an obsession. For me, seeing pornography was like lighting a fuse on a stick of dynamite. I became stimulated and had to gratify my urges and explode...If pornographic material would have been unavailable to me in my early stages, it is most probable that my sexual activities would not have escalated to the degree they did."

During his trial, the jurors listened to Bishop's taped confession that included admissions that he had molested his victims after their deaths. During the confession he giggled at times, mimicked the final words of some of his victims in a high falsetto voice, and also said that he was glad he was caught because he would have done it again.

Bishop also confessed that his offering help to Mrs. Cunningham was, in fact genuine. He wanted to allay her despair but did not know how to tell her that he had killed her son.

Ultimately, Bishop was convicted of five counts of murder, five counts of kidnapping, and one count of sexual abuse of a minor. Jude Jay Banks condemned Bishop from the bench and told him that state law gave Bishop the choice of execution by firing squad or lethal injection. Without hesitation he chose the latter.

Bishop later wrote a letter to explain his motives, reiterating much of what he said in his interview. He wrote:

"I am a homosexual pedophile convicted of murder, and pornography was a determining factor in my downfall. Somehow I became sexually attracted to young boys and I would fantasize about them naked. Certain bookstores offered sex education, photographic, or art books which occasionally contained pictures of nude boys. I purchased such books and used them to enhance my masturbatory fantasies...Finding and procuring sexually arousing materials became an obsession. For me, seeing pornography was lighting a fuse on a stick of dynamite. I became

stimulated and had to gratify my urges or explode. All boys became mere sexual objects. My conscience was desensitized and my sexual appetite entirely controlled my actions."

Soon after Bishop was sentenced, while on death row at the Utah State Prison at Point of the Mountain, there was a rumor that some unknown people had offered a $5,000 bounty for his murder, as well as another $5,000 for his brother Douglas' head. Prison Security Chief Captain Craig Rasmussen told reporters that these types of rumors occur pretty regularly but they had to take the threats against Bishop seriously because if he were to be attacked or otherwise injured after they had been given the warning then catastrophic results could ensue. There were no attempts on the lives of either of the Bishop brothers; however, their status as "short eyes" (child molesters) rendered them both outcasts within the prison hierarchy.

During this time Bishop was trying to rectify his Mormon beliefs with his current status. He said, "With great sadness and remorse, I realize that I allowed myself to be misled by Satan." This rediscovery of his religion led to a sort of repentance and some hope that he might actually survive, albeit in prison. His attorneys pursued a petition for a new trial but on 3 February 1988 the Utah Supreme Court rejected these efforts. At this time Bishop did, in fact, give up hope and resign himself to death.

On 29 February, Bishop filed a motion to dismiss his attorneys and to replace them with counsel who would be willing to abandon any further appeals. Following another competency hearing, the trial court determined that Bishop knew what he was doing and on 2 May the Utah Supreme Court lifted his indefinite stay of execution and ordered the trial court to set an execution date.

Three days later, Bishop appeared in front of Judge Frank Noel—handcuffed and shackled—and read a brief handwritten statement that said:

"In reflecting back on my life, I remember a lot of good things, but these are overshadowed by the things I have done. I wish I could make restitution somehow, but I don't see how I can. I wish I could go back and change what happened, or that by giving my life these five innocent lives could be restored. Again, I say that I am truly sorry for all the anguish."

Judge Noel was unmoved by Bishop's words and signed his official death warrant, scheduling Bishop's execution for 10 June 1988.

Just prior to his execution, prison psychologist Al Carlisle told reporters that Bishop appeared to be a new man who had read the *Book of Mormon* ten times from cover-to-cover during his four years in prison and wore television headphones to drown out the profanity spewed at him by other inmates. Carlisle also stated that Bishop feared that his old impulses would return if he were ever freed. He added that Bishop demonstrated remorse during his entire time in prison and that Bishop believed that he would be entering the spirit world which will be more peaceful than on Earth. He also stated that Bishop didn't believe that he had been forgiven but he did believe that he could continue to work on his problems "on the other side."

Bishop then told prison officials and guards that he was "ready and anxious to die."

Bishop met with his parents for the final time on 8 June 1988 and then spent the remainder of his time alive by fasting and praying. Mormon Bishop Heber Geurts told *Salt Lake Tribune* reporter Robert Mims that it was unbelievable how calm and cool Bishop was during his final moments alive. Geurts added, "Even the guards can't understand it. I've dealt with thousands of inmates in 33 years, and he's the most sorrowful and repentant and remorseful man I've ever seen."

Whereas Bishop appeared to absolve his soul through his realignment with the Mormon Church and did, in fact, appear on all accounts to be extremely repentant, this neither eliminates nor minimizes the fact that he purposefully abducted five young boys, sexually assaulted them, and then murdered them; in addition to countless other children who he had sexually molested. These five boys are gone forever and their families are left to suffer their losses and Bishop's other victims had their innocence stolen from them; something they will never be able to recover. At least his own recognition of his deviant pedophiliac proclivities and push to stop any and all appeals in order to reach the death chamber as soon as possible did, in fact, serve to save an unknown number of other potential victims.

By 8:00 p.m. Wednesday, 8 June, Bishop had been transferred from his maximum security death row cell to a holding cell a mere 100 feet from the death chamber and, as is commonplace, was placed under 24-hour observation.

Twenty-seven hours later—just before midnight on Friday 10 June, Bishop was escorted into the 24-foot-by-24-foot execution chamber "with practiced precision." He was shackled yet did not resist, fully cooperating with the corrections officers. He was directed to climb onto the gurney that was bolted to the concrete floor in the northwest corner of the room and to stretch out his arms. Bishop did so without any hesitation. Utah Department of Corrections Deputy Director Bruce Egan stated that while Bishop was relaxed about the prospect of dying he was, in fact, "very nervous" about the execution itself.

Bishop forewent the "traditional" last statement to, first, dispel any rumors that he had been sexually molested as a child or had committed other murders and, second, to pray for his fellow man. Bishop said:

"By accepting my execution I do not consider myself a courageous hero or a noble martyr, or that I am giving up or that I'm going out in a blaze of glory, as some people have suggested. I am merely accepting my just punishment as my conscience dictates I must. Though perhaps too little too late, I am doing the right thing now."

As well as:

"I leave this life with no ill feelings towards anyone, and I pray that the peace of God may rest upon each and every one of you. I know of God's

love, patience and compassion, and have found comfort in that knowledge. When I kneel before Christ in the next life, having a perfect recollection of all my guilt, with a broken heart, I will humbly plead, 'Jesus, thou Son of God, have mercy on my soul.'"

Arthur Gary Bishop was ultimately executed smoothly and without flaw on Friday, 10 June 1988. At the time of his execution he expressed remorse for his actions.

By 12:15 a.m.—a mere nine minutes after his execution began—Bishop was pronounced dead by Dr. J. Brett Lazar, director of the Division of Community Health Services. Bishop's body was then taken to the state medical examiner's office for an autopsy before it was released to his family for the cremation Bishop requested.

Aftermath

Interestingly, the fact that Utah offers its condemned prisoners the choice of death by firing squad or lethal injection dates back to the early days of the Mormon Church in the 1850s when Brigham Young and Heber Kimball preached a doctrine of strict "blood atonement." This meant that sinners could demonstrate their repentance by spilling their own blood and if they failed to do so then other church members may be required to assist them. Thankfully, that grim doctrine is largely ignored today except by extremists such as Ervil LeBaron—dubbed the "Mormon Manson"—whose mass-murdering polygamist cult continues to practice it. Double killer Gary Gilmore chose the firing squad for his own execution in 1977 and continues to be the last to choose said method; however, the option remains on the books.

THE BRILLIANT SERIAL KILLER : THE TRUE STORY OF ISRAEL KEYES

MARK TOLBERT

Israel Keyes was an American serial killer who was active from approximately 2001 to his capture in 2012. He was known for his extreme attention to detail, his patience and discipline in selecting targets that lived far away from him. He was also meticulous in disposing of his victim's bodies as authorities have not uncovered any other evidence that Keyes did not provide.

Keyes killed several victims across the United States and was finally caught in 2012 after he uncharacteristically deviated from his modus operandi and hatched a plan to collect a ransom from his last victim's family.

Keyes was known to go to extreme lengths to hide his involvement in these murders, including driving across the country in rental cars, while using nothing but cash and removing the batteries from his cell phones in order to evade detection. This is uncharacteristic for a serial killer, since the vast majority of his contemporaries are known to have killed within their general geographic area.

While in federal custody in Anchorage, Alaska, Keyes would cooperate with investigators and admit to a host of crimes, including kidnapping, rape, and murder. Furthermore, Keyes admitted to committing a variety of burglaries and bank robberies to fund his killing sprees.

Early Life

Israel Keyes was born in Richmond, Utah in 1978. He was the second child to John Jeffrey Keyes and Heidi Hokansson. John, a maintenance man, and Heidi, a stay-at-home mom, raised their son in a Mormon environment and home-schooled both Israel and his eight siblings.

Soon after his birth, Israel's parents moved the family to Aladdin Road, a small area north of Colville, Washington. While his family officially followed the Mormon faith, they were known to attend a local Christian Identity church, an organization rumored follow a white supremacist version of Christianity. Some, however, dispute this label and liken the religion to having parallels with the Amish church.

The family also quickly became friends with the neighbors, the Kehoe family. Chevie Kehoe, the eldest of eight sons, would later become an infamous white supremacist and convicted murderer, after killing William Frederick Mueller, along with his wife and daughter, during a robbery to secure guns, ammunition, and money.

During his time in Aladdin Road, Israel became a very introverted child with little interaction with the other children in town. He built his own cabin at the age of sixteen and preferred the wilderness over people. He is known to have burglarized several houses during his time in Aladdin, however, and is believed to have killed family pets for entertainment.

"When I was fourteen there was some friends staying with us," Keyes recalled. "And there was this cat of ours that was always getting into the trash. I had a lot of guns and I would always carry a gun and I shot it in the stomach. And it ran around and around the tree...and then it like crashed into the tree. I actually kind of laughed a little I think but..and then I looked over at everybody else and the kid who was with me, he was throwing up. Like he was, really, I don't know (chuckles) traumatized I guess you would say."

"Like most serial killers," forensic psychiatrist Paula Orange said. "Keyes built himself up to killing people by killing small animals first."

Following his family's relocation to Smyrna, Maine to become involved in the maple syrup business in the late 1990s, Keyes was kicked out of his family home for rejecting his parents' faith. His parents told his siblings to stay away from him.

"Keyes didn't think too much of his family," Orange said. "He was raised in a cult-like atmosphere and rejected the family religion, becoming very outspoken out his lack of belief in God. He had a Satanic pentagram branded on his back as well as an upside-down cross on his chest."

The rejection made Keyes want to tour the country and burn down as many churches as he could. Instead, he turned to murder and rape.

His first violent crime was committed sometime between 1996 and 1998, when Keyes abducted a teenage girl and raped her. Despite his later penchant for murder, he allowed this victim to go free. The identity of the teenage girl remains unknown.

Military Career

In 1998, Israel Keyes decided to enlist in the United States Army while living in New Jersey. Keyes served as a specialist in the 1st Battalion, 5th Infantry. He was subsequently stationed at Ft. Lewis, near Tacoma, Washington, and at Ft. Hood, near Killeen, Texas. He would later receive training in the Sinai region of Egypt.

While serving in the U.S. Army, Keyes was awarded the Army Achievement Medal for "meritorious service while assigned as a gunner and assistant gunner from the 2nd of December 1998 to the 8th of July, 2001 in the Alpha Company 60mm mortar section." Although Keyes received a DUI in Washington state in May 2001, he left the U.S. Army with an honorable discharge later that year.

Keyes would settle in Alaska and get a job working in construction. Incredibly, he would draw rave reviews from his employer who had no idea of the double life his new carpenter with the long hair led.

"Keyes was described as someone who was very professional," Orange said. "He had a tremendous focus and would work on projects for hours on end with intensity and focus. He would not stop for lunch. He would just work straight on through."

Keyes was described in a favorable manner by just about everyone else who met him. Words like "friendly", "low-key", "reliable" were among the adjectives used to describe him.

"The secret life was power to Israel Keyes," Orange said. "He got off on the fact that everyone he encountered had no idea who or what he really was. To them, he was a friendly carpenter who was on the quiet side. Mellow. But inside he was a raging killer. That is what gave him power."

Crimes

Bill & Lorraine Currier

After receiving his honorable discharge from the United States Army, and sometime between April and May 2011, Israel Keyes constructed a homemade silencer for his Ruger .22 pistol. Once he decided to kill, Keyes booked a flight from Washington state to Indiana. After arriving in Indiana, Keyes rented a car and drove the remaining 1,000 miles to the East Coast of the United States, using cash-only for the duration of the trip to avoid leaving behind any evidence.

Keyes arrived in New York to test his homemade silencer, then traveled to Vermont to pick up a murder "toolkit" that he had buried two years before. Keyes soon found an abandoned farmhouse in Essex, Vermont, which he identified as the location he would take his next victim to before killing them. He initially targeted random drivers passing through the rural area, intending to shoot out a tire on their car and kidnap them after they crashed, but decided to focus on a married couple after dismissing his original plan as unpractical and dangerous.

He soon identified Bill and Lorraine Currier, living at 8 Colbert Street, as his next victims on July 8, 2011.

Bill and Lorraine were 49 and 55 years old respectively. They had just celebrated their 25th wedding anniversary. Bill worked at the local university as a lab assistant while Lorraine worked at a nearby medical center.

"They were good people," Orange said. "They had a lot of pride in the upkeep of their Vermont home, manicuring the lawn and planting flowers. They were good employees and well-liked by co-workers. They were the epitome of upstanding, normal good people."

Keyes had picked the Currier's because they had no dog, no kids and a garage that would let him into the house. He stalked them for days, knowing their comings and going.

As one investigator would note, "Keyes was a serial killer with a system."

In the middle of the night, Keyes disabled the Currier's phone line and entered their house in what has been described as a "blitz attack." He ambushed the couple while they were sleeping and quickly subdued them, tying the couple up and stealing Lorraine's .38 snub-nose revolver in the process.

Once the couple was secured, he proceeded to transport them to the abandoned farmhouse in Essex. During the course of the night, both Lorraine and Bill attempted to escape the house. Lorraine was successfully captured and re-restrained. However, Keyes shot Bill with his silenced .22 caliber Ruger pistol in a fit of rage during his escape attempt. After killing Bill, Keyes sexually assaulted Lorraine and strangled her to death in the basement.

Following the killings, Keyes buried Bill and Lorraine's bodies in the basement of the Essex farmhouse, intending to return to the house at a later date to set fire to the building and thereby destroy any evidence in the blaze. Once the bodies were buried, Keyes set out to commit a robbery spree using the Currier's car.

"Keyes was spotted driving the Currier's car," Orange said. "The eyewitness quickly relayed this information to the police and they were able to come up with a sketch of Keyes. They were reported missing by this time and the authorities knew that foul play was involved. Things became particularly worrisome as the man in Currier's car was driving alone and the couple was nowhere to be found."

The Currier's car soon suffered "serious mechanical issues" and Keyes decided not to go through with his crime spree.

Keyes quickly abandoned the Currier's non working car in an apartment parking lot at 203 Pearl Street and proceeded to the White National Monument Forest to burn the couple's belongings and to bury his toolkit and handgun.

Unbeknownst to Keyes, the farmhouse containing the Currier's bodies was bulldozed from October 25-27, 2011. The bodies, along with the rest of the farmhouse, were unknowingly disposed of at the local landfill.

The resting place lived up to Keyes' motto, 'Out of sight, out of mind.'

Samantha Koenig

On February 1, 2012, Keyes began to search for another random victim. He identified 18-year old barista Samantha Koenig, living and working in Anchorage, Alaska, as his next victim.

Samantha worked at a walk-up kiosk on a relatively busy highway. It was snowing that night, however, and folks were driving by too fast to pay attention to the man who walked up to the counter in a ski mask. This would not be unusual in Anchorage as the weather was freezing. Samantha greeted Israel with a smile and he handed her his travel mug, asking for some coffee. She would turn back around he had a gun pointed at her.

"Turn out the lights," he commanded.

Samantha complied.

"Turn around," he said.

Samantha began to cry, complying with his command. He forced her to empty the register then tied up her wrists with cable wire. After finding out that Koenig had a boyfriend who was set to show up soon, Keyes laid in wait for the boyfriend, Duane Tortolani. However, he quickly abandoned his plan to capture a second victim and dragged Koenig to his truck before transporting her to his property.

The next day, February 2nd, Keyes broke into Koenig's house. While there, he also burglarized her boyfriend's truck, taking the couple's joint debit card with him. However, both Koenig's father and Duane Tortolani witnessed this burglary and notified the authorities.

Keyes quickly tested the debit card to make sure that it worked and, upon confirming that it worked, he returned to his home and quickly killed Koenig, leaving her body in a storage shed located on his property. He immediately traveled to New Orleans, where he set out on a week-long cruise. However, once he disembarked from the cruise Keyes became increasingly concerned over the media coverage and intense police investigation of Keonig's disappearance and set out on a crime spree.

On February 16, Keyes burglarized and burned down a home in Aledo, Texas. Shortly thereafter, Keyes robbed the National Bank of Texas, attempting to kidnap yet another woman he saw walking a dog. Luckily, this potential victim was able to escape.

Other Victims

Israel Keyes is suspected of killing or attempting to kill several other victims. Keyes' first admitted violent crime took place sometime between 1996 and 1998, when he abducted and raped a teenage girl in Washington state. Unlike his later crimes, Keyes did not kill this victim. He released her soon after the sexual assault.

"My entire goal was to stay under the radar," Keyes said. "For a lot of this stuff, there wasn't anything. All I can say is that unless I talk about it, you're never going to find any evidence."

His first suspected murder is of an unknown couple in Washington State in 2001. Keyes also claimed to have killed another unidentified victim in Leah Bay, Washington in July 2001.

He planned out his killings like most people plan out their vacations. He would travel far away from his location.

From 2005 to 2006, Keyes is suspected of killing two separate victims. He confessed to these murders while being held at the

Anchorage Correctional Complex, saying that these murders were committed on two separate occasions. Furthermore, he claimed to have dumped one of the bodies in Crescent Lake, located in Oregon.

"There is a history of this stuff that goes back a long time," Keyes said. "It's not something I've ever talked to anyone about."

Keyes just didn't rape his female victims. He would rape his male victims as well. It was something he was ashamed of as well as his necrophilia.

Following a multi-year break from killing, Keyes admitted to killing Debra J. Feldman in Hackensack, New Jersey on April 8, 2009. He also claimed to have killed another victim the following day somewhere in New York state.

Keyes would bury his murder weapons across numerous fields across the entire United States. Because of his military training, he knew how to maintain the weapons and return to them after they had been out of use for years. He buried these weapons in canisters filled with cable ties, ropes and drain cleaner.

During these trips, Keyes would admit to frequenting prostitutes.

Lastly, following the murder of Samantha Koenig and during his travels throughout the Southwestern United States, Keyes claims to have killed an unknown victim in Texas. The identity and final location of this victim remain unknown.

In addition to the actual murders that he committed, Keyes admitted to attempting to kill several other individuals over the years. For example, Keyes admitted to attempting to shoot both a couple and male police officer in Anchorage, Alaska sometime between April and May 2011. He also admitted to attempting to kidnap and kill a woman he spotted walking her dog in Texas, just days before his capture by a combination of Texas and federal law enforcement.

Other Crimes

Keyes was known to commit burglaries and bank robberies in order to fund his killing sprees. In addition, he admitted to killing small animals from the time he was a young child. He is said to have killed an unknown number of family dogs and cats throughout his travels.

<u>April 10, 2009</u>

Keyes robbed the Community Bank in Tupper Lake, NY in order to fund his killing spree. After holding up the bank teller with a .40 caliber Smith & Wesson (and with a .22 caliber 10/22 Ruger pistol in reserve), Keyes made off with over $10,000 in cash. Although he was filmed on camera during the robbery, his use of sunglasses, uncharacteristic clothing, and a fake mustache prevented him from being identified.

Following the successful robbery, Keyes buried a box with his robbery supplies in the Woodside Natural Area in Essex, Utah. He returned home four days later with the $10,000 in his possession.

<u>February 16, 2012</u>

While Keyes was traversing across the Southwestern United States following the successful ransom for Samantha Koenig, he committed two additional crimes. First, Keyes committed arson by setting fire to and burning down a 3,500 square foot house in Aledo, Texas. Secondly, Keyes again committed a bank robbery by holding up a teller at the National Bank of Texas in Azle, Texas, making off with an undisclosed amount of cash.

In all, Keyes is suspected of committing some 20 to 30 home invasions and burglaries during his lifetime. Furthermore, he killed an unknown amount of animals from his childhood to capture and is believed to have committed several unidentified bank robberies during his adult years in order to fund his killing trips across the country.

Capture

After murdering Samantha Koenig and leaving Alaska, Keyes concocted a plan to demand a $30,000 ransom for Koenig's return (at the time, police were unaware that Koenig had been killed). Keyes texted his demands and instructions to Duane Tortolani, Koenig's boyfriend.

At the same time, Keyes dug up the body of Samantha Koenig, dismembered it, and disposed of the body in Matanuska Lake.

The case became a high-profile one and community members chipped in to meet the ransom demand.

Thirty-thousand dollars, courtesy of a concerned and frightened community, would be deposited into Samantha's account.

After receiving the ransom money, Keyes began withdrawing cash from the associated account using her stolen debit card. There would be withdrawals in Alaska. Then Arizona. Then New Mexico.

The authorities would always be fifteen minutes behind the suspect when he made these withdrawals.

Israel would wear a "Scream" mask while the withdrawals but his 2012 Ford Focus that he was drawing was identified. The FBI noted all of their counterparts to be on the lookout for Keyes in this vehicle. It is important to note that Keyes actually exchanged his rented 2012 Ford Focus for another car to avoid detection; however, the rental company provided him with another 2012 Ford Focus for his exchange. This would eventually help to lead to his capture.

Police were then able to track account withdrawals as he traveled throughout the Southwestern United States, having made withdrawals from Koenig's account using her debit card in New Mexico, Arizona, and Texas. Interestingly, authorities had a video of Koenig's abduction but refused to release the footage to the public, a controversial move that many outsiders saw as hampering his capture.

Having left his sister's wedding just days before (where he became embroiled in a contentious argument about his pronounced atheism), Keyes was spotted speeding along Highway 59 by a Texas Highway Patrolman on March 13, 2012.

"The patrolman that made the traffic stop had no idea that Keyes was a wanted serial killer," Orange said "Keyes did not have his gun handy at the time. If he had, there's no doubt in my mind that he would have started shooting."

Keyes was placed under arrest by the patrolman and the Texas Rangers as well as the FBI was brought in. Authorities found the following items in Keyes' possession at the time of his capture: Koenig's ATM card and cell phone (with the battery removed), a ski-mask, handgun, and bundles of rubber-banded cash that was traced to the recent National Bank of Texas robbery.

The authorities still had hope that Samantha was still alive.

But Keyes would tell them nothing. He stared straight ahead without emotion as detectives hammered him with questions. Authorities would get very little out of him. He was thirty-four years old and lived a quiet life with his girlfriend and ten year old daughter in Anchorage. Everything about Keyes' past seemed normal. But he had a creepy withdrawn nature about his personality. When the FBI searched his property, they found out why.

He had searched numerous time on his computer for Samantha Koenig. The FBI would then confront Keyes with the surveillance footage they had of his truck pulling up in front of the kiosk.

"We know it was your truck," the FBI agent said.

Keyes would remain silent for about forty seconds before he finally spoke.

"Well, I might as well tell you everything. She's dead."

Keyes revealed that he had used a needle and thread to open up Samantha's eyes as she posed with the newspaper in the ransom photo.

Keyes would recount how he brought Samantha back to his home and tied her up. He had a glass of wine before he began verbally taunting Samantha by telling her what he was going to do to her. He then raped the victim and choked her to death.

Only twenty feet away, his live-in girlfriend and ten year old daughter were sleeping. They would wake up the following morning and he would join them at the breakfast table. Like turning a switch on-and-off, he spoke of taking his family on a cruise.

"It was apparent that neither his girlfriend or his daughter knew of his crimes," Orange said. "He would tell investigators that 'no one really knew him.'"

Shortly after Keyes' capture in Lufkin, he was then extradited to Alaska to stand trial for Koenig's murder. His trial was set for March 2013 and he was slated to be represented by federal defender Rich Curtner. Keyes was thirty-four years old at the time of his arrest.

Investigation

Israel Keyes was officially extradited to Alaska on March 26, 2012. Shortly after arriving at the Anchorage Correctional Complex, Keyes confessed to the murder of Samantha Koenig, providing information which allowed investigators to locate her dismembered body on April 1st of the same year.

Keyes was initially willing to cooperate with authorities and offered to confess and plead guilty to all charges leveled against him if two terms were met: his trial would last no longer than one year and he would be given the death penalty. He also conditioned his cooperation on the basis that his name and certain details not be released to the media and public.

"I'm not in this for the glory," Keyes told interrogators. "I'm not trying to be on TV. I want my kid to have a chance to grow up. She's in a safe place now, she's not going to see any of this. I want her to have a chance to grow up and not have this hanging over her head."

In June 2012, Keyes attempted to violently escape from a courthouse in Anchorage, in what authorities suspected was a spur-of-the-moment suicide attempt. Keyes was successfully subdued with a taser and taken back into custody alive. Following his attempted escape, Keyes was placed on a suicide watch, which entailed a prohibition on razor blades and sharp objects, regular inspections of his cell, and a 24/7 guard.

The next month, in July 2012, a local news station, WCAX, reported Keyes' connection to the kidnapping and murder of the

Curriers. This lead to Keyes ending all cooperation with the authorities for the next two months.

Modus Operandi

While cooperating with authorities at the Anchorage Correctional Complex, Keyes described his approach to killing thusly: "I would let them come to me... You might not get exactly what you're looking for, there's not much to pick from, so to speak. But there's also no witnesses, there's nobody else around."

Location

Israel Keyes was very methodical in his approach to killing. Unlike most serial killers, Keyes did not kill victims who lived near him. Most serial killers conduct most of their kidnapping and abductions within the vicinity of their home, which leads to an easier investigation and higher chance of being captured. Keyes, on the other hand, was known to take cross-country trips in order to kill.

For example, Keyes killed the Curriers in Vermont while he was living in Washington state. Once he decided to kill, Keyes booked a flight from Washington to Indiana. He then rented a car, removed the battery from his cell phone, and paid for all of his expenses with cash as he drove 1,000 miles to the East Coast. He tested his homemade silencer in New York, retrieved a murder toolkit that he had hidden in Vermont two years earlier, and then identified the Curriers as his next victims. This type of careful planning, attention to detail, and restraint is very uncommon in serial killers.

Victim Profile

Unlike most serial killers, Keyes did not have a specific victim profile. For instance, Ted Bundy, another serial killer who shared many qualities with Keyes, was known to target young, white women between the ages of 15 and 25. However, Keyes had no such victim profile. He alternatively killed or attempted to kill married couples, young woman, men, and several other unknown victims. This allowed him to operate without substantial police scrutiny for some time.

Method of Killing

With the exception of his killing of Bill Currier, Keyes strangled every one of his victims. Furthermore, Bill Currier was shot to death while attempting to escape from the house that Keyes was keeping him and his wife at. Had Bill not been killed in the heat of passion while attempting to escape, it is likely that Keyes eventually would have strangled him to death as well.

Death

After accidentally being provided with razors while on suicide watch, Keyes committed suicide on December 2nd, 2012. He sliced his wrists vertically and hung himself while being held at the Anchorage Correctional Complex. He was pronounced dead immediately.

Prior to committing suicide, Keyes composed a four-page, handwritten letter that was found underneath his body. The letter was covered in blood and was largely illegible, but FBI forensic investigators were able to reconstruct much of his letter.

While the letter did not provide additional details about his crimes and victims, it did offer a glimpse into his psyche and reasons for committing murders. Keyes wrote "Family and friends will shed a few tears, pretend it's off to heaven you go. But the reality is you were just bones and meat, and with your brain died also your soul." Later in his letter he elaborated, "You may have been free, you loved living your lie, fate had its own scheme crushed like a bug, you still die." He repeatedly referred to his victims as a "pretty captive butterfly."

Dr. Stephen Montgomery, a forensic psychiatrist at Vanderbilt University Medical Center analyzed the letter and reached the following conclusion: "It has no remorse, no regard for human life or the victims and that fits with that type of psychopathic personality."

Authorities are still investigating various unsolved disappearances throughout the various states that Keyes visited. It is now believed that he may have targeted homeless shelters where he could kill people who would not be missed.

The Texarkana Moonlight Murders

77

IRIS HULSE

Texarkana has always been an unusual place. On the east, you have Texarkana, Arkansas, a small town by any other measurement, yet home to the largest population in Miller County. To the west lies Texarkana, Texas, located in rural Bowie County and lucky enough to have its very own Wal-Mart. Together these twin cities make up what is simply referred to as "Texarkana."

Texarkana is a dusty town, built on a foundation of competing railroads and a Mexican border dispute in the 1800s. The town laid low for the next several years, sending off its sons to fight World War I and then II, and welcoming them back home for better or for worse. But no one in Texarkana was prepared for the national attention that came in the spring of 1946. On February 22nd, 1946, a masked serial killer, dubbed the "Phantom Killer" by the *Texarkana Gazette*'s Calvin Sutton, began terrorizing young couples on the town's secluded country roads.

Today, if you search the Internet for information on Texarkana and its morbid history, you will likely be redirected to pages on *The Town That Dreaded Sundown* and its Arkansan producer, Charles B. Pierce. In 1977, decades after the last murders, this film joined the ranks of *Halloween* and *The Texas Chainsaw Massacre* as one of Hollywood's classic horrors, featuring countless local residents as set extras. While the film's accuracy is something to be questioned, it remains a key piece of the town's identity. Visitors can even catch a screening every Halloween at Spring Lake Park, not far from where one of the infamous murders took place.

Texarkana may have embraced its celebrity status, but eighty years ago the town was paralyzed in fear. Within a single spring, five were dead and three were wounded. All in what had previously been a quiet, friendly community.

A Masked Attacker

Just before midnight, on February 22nd, 1946, Jimmy Hollis and Mary Jeanne Larey were finishing up their date in the backseat of

Hollis' father's car. Hollis, 24, and Larey, 19, had been dating for a while, but his parents expected the car (and the lovebirds) home by midnight. Throwing caution to the wind, they parked on a secluded dirt road, known as a lovers' lane, and proceeded to do what young couples will do.

The pair was soon startled by a flashlight, shining through the driver side window and blinding them to whoever stood outside. Hollis quickly composed himself and opened the door, thinking they were being interrupted by an ill-timed police patrol or a prank from some local kids, but they found themselves face-to-face with a masked man holding a gun.

Hollis continued to confront the intruder, telling him, "Fellow, you've got me mixed up with someone else. You got the wrong man." Hollis later said that the masked man muttered something like, "I don't want to kill you, so do what I say." Hollis attempted to calm the assailant, who forced the young man out of the vehicle and demanded Hollis remove his pants, gun pointed squarely at his face. Larey pleaded with Hollis to do as the man said, thinking he would not become violent if they did as he said. Instead the masked man overpowered Hollis, beating him over the head with the revolver. As Hollis lay limp on the cold ground, the attack continued until the sound of Hollis' skull cracking echoed throughout the clearing.

At this point Larey was hysterical with panic, thinking the loud crack of Hollis' broken skull was the sound of him being shot. She told the man they had no money or valuables, attempting to hand the man Hollis' wallet, but he only screamed, "Liar," at her and demanded her purse. Then the masked man told her to run toward the road. Larey ran as fast as she could, but the strange man pursued, continuing to scream, "Liar," at her as she ran.

The assailant eventually outpaced Larey, and forced her to the ground. Larey reported that the man did not rape her, but that assaulted her violent and used his gun to sexually molest her. Larey was afraid for her life, fighting against the weight of her attacker. She eventually managed to escape his grasp, rising up and telling him, "Go ahead and kill me." She then ran to a nearby house at 805 Blanton Street, where she managed to wake up the sleeping woners and pleaded for help. Shortly after, the Bowie County Sheriff, W.H. "Bill" Presley, arrived at what would be the first known Phantom Killer crime scene.

Hollis and Larey were lucky enough to survive this first attack, though they were left with plenty of physical and emotional scars to show for it. Hollis and Larey described their attacker as a tall man wearing a burlap sack with two slits cut for the eyes, though they could not agree on the man's race. Hollis believed the man was white, with tanned skin from working outdoors, while Larey insisted he was a black man because of his mannerisms and "curses." At this point, the attack was treated as a random attempted robbery, it was unknown the chaos that the Phantom Killer would bring in coming months.

The First Kill

In the early hours of March 24th, a truck driver spotted a young man asleep in an Oldsmobile parked on the side of the road. Concerned about the danger of passing traffic, the truck driver ran up to the window, hoping to wake the man and advise him of a better resting area. To the truck driver's horror, the young man was not asleep; he had been shot twice in the back of the head and sat dead in the driver's seat. In the Oldsmobile's backseat was a teenage girl wrapped in a bloody blanket, her body was completely lifeless. These young lovers were not as lucky as the Phantom Killer's first victims.

Richard Griffin, 29, was a retired Navy SeaBee on a double date with his girlfriend of six weeks, Polly Ann Moore, 17, when they pulled over on the highway to have some time alone. They had just finished up dinner with Griffin's sister and her boyfriend at a local café, and Griffin was in no rush to return his girlfriend to her parents' house. Unfortunately, they would never make it home.

Sometime that previous night, Griffin and Moore had pulled over onto the side of the road. It is believed they were approached similarly to the Phantom Killer's first victims, with a blinding flashlight and pointed gun. There was a heavy rainfall over Texarkana that night, so no one would have been out and about to see the killings take place.

Griffin was likely killed first, with two shots from a .32 Colt revolver to the back of his head. Moore, however, had been dragged from the vehicle and sexually assaulted on the cold, wet ground by their attacker. Blood and marks littered the dirt next to the vehicle. After this horror, Moore was also shot and killed by the Phantom Killer. The assailant pulled a blanket from the car's trunk and wrapped her in it before placing her body in the backseat of the Oldsmobile. Any fingerprints and footprints left behind by the killer that night was washed away by the storm.

Griffin's pockets were found empty and turned inside out, and Moore's purse remained at the scene but was emptied of any cash. With the only apparent motive being robbery, questions still remained as to why the crime was carried out so violently. The *Texarkana Gazette*, at the insistence of the Sheriff Bill Presley, made an announcement on March 27th asking residents to not spread rumors or anything else that they did not see with their own two eyes. Despite offering a cash reward, no solid tips ever made it to the police force.

Murder in the Park

Betty Jo Booker, 15, was a straight-A student who was adored by those around her. She worked with Jerry Atkins playing saxophone for a local band, The Rhythmaires, every Saturday night at the local VFW club. On April 14th, she and Atkins, as well as the rest of their band mates, were playing one of their normal shows. Every other weekend, Atkins gave Booker a ride home alternating with a band mate named Ernie Holcomb. This night was Holcomb's night to drive her home, but Booker told Holcomb not to bother because she had a ride set up with an old classmate who was visiting, Paul Martin. Atkins never knew of this change of plans, and until he received a call the next morning he assumed Booker had left with Holcombe, as usual.

Martin's 1946 Ford Coupe was found at 6:30 the next morning by the Weaver family, who were on their way through Texarkana to Prescott, Arkansas. The keys were found still in the car's ignition. Several miles away, in Spring Lake Park, their bodies would be found. Neither the car nor their bodies were anywhere near their destination that night.

Band and classmates claimed that the two were never close to being a couple, and that Booker felt obligated to go out with Martin because of their connection at school. However, no one knows what they were doing pulled over that night, or why they were in that area of town in the first place. No matter what the true story was that night, Booker and Martin would be the Phantom Killer's third and fourth victims.

Like the previous attack, both victims were shot and killed with a .32 Colt semi-automatic revolver. And like the female targets before her, Booker had been sexually assaulted before her murder. After news of the murder was released, hundreds of Texarkana residents flooded the park, hoping to catch a glimpse of the crime scene or help the investigation.

Martin's body was found almost a mile and a half from the abandoned car. He had been shot four times and the ground surrounding his body was covered in his blood.

Booker's body would not be found until five hours later, over three miles from where the car had been found. Booker was found by the Boyd family and Ted Schoeppey, who had joined the community search party to help find the two teenage victims. Booker had been shot twice, and was found with her hand in her coat pocket.

Both bodies showed signs of a struggle against their attacker, yet their fight was unsuccessful. There was no conclusive evidence as to why their bodies were so far from their car.

Booker's missing saxophone played in the running theory of robbery as a primary motive. The police had alerts al over the area, asking people to keep an eye out for a pawned or for sale saxophone matching the serial number of Booker's, and for several months it was considered one of the best leads the authorities had on finding the

killer. Unfortunately for the police, on October 24th, six months after Booker's murder, P. V. Ward and J. F. McNief found the saxophone still in its leather case, just yards from where Booker's body had been found. Ward claimed to know what it was as soon as they stumbled upon it. By the time the case and instrument were turned over to the police, the case had already been labeled closed.

A Red Herring

Public panic over the Phantom Killer was at its all-time high when Virgil and Katie Starks were attacked in their modest farmhouse just ten miles out of town. However, questions would eventually emerge over whether this was truly the work of the Phantom Killer, or if someone else was responsible for the crime.

On the quiet night of May 3^{rd,} Virgil, 36, was reading the Texarkana Gazette when two gunshots burst through the front window of their ranch-style home. These bullets hit Virgil in the head, killing him instantly. Katie was lying in bed, already dressed in her nightgown, when she heard the sound of breaking glass. She headed for the living room, where her husband had been seated, only to find him slumped in his armchair, dead. She cried in fear as she reached for the phone, but the attacker shot through her lower jaw, spraying teeth fragments across the Starks kitchen.

In a state of panic and extreme pain, Katie managed to get back up to her feet. She attempted to grab her husband's gun, but was disoriented from being shot. Despite her injuries, she escaped from the house and ran for her sister's down the street. Finding the house empty, she continued to her neighbors' until she found refuge in the Prater house, where the police were finally called. When A. V. Prater answered the door, Katie simply said, "Virgil's dead," before collapsing on the ground. In the time it took for the police to arrive the killer had fled, taking no valuables or anything else of note with him.

Initially, this attack was labeled as another of the Phantom Killer's. It followed the same time pattern as his previous attacks, used a gun as the primary weapon, and targeted a couple. One of the biggest pieces of evidence connecting this attack to the Phantom Killer was a set of unfamiliar tire tracks that matched those found at the other crime scenes. Because of these similarities, many citizens of Texarkana insist that this murder and attempted assault was the Phantom Killer's final blow to the small town's community.

In November 1948, the local authorities made a different conclusion. Another man was arrested and charged with the home invasion and attack on Virgil and Katie Starks. Law enforcement referenced several reasons as to this not being the work of the Phantom Killer, including the fact that the weapon used was a .22 rifle. This change in weapon, as well as the fact this was a home invasion earlier in the evening, pointed police to consider a different suspect entirely.

The town is still home to many skeptics who believe this attack was the Phantom Killer's doing. The crime scene at the Starks home was filled with physical DNA evidence, but at the time DNA testing was only beginning to emerge in the most developed areas of the nation. A little town like Texarkana was nowhere near equipped to handle a case like this, and the DNA evidence was discarded or improperly stored for later testing. While the official stance is that the Phantom Killer was not involved in this attack, the question still haunts many in the area.

A Town In Panic

As the attacks added up, tension in the town of Texarkana grew. After the first and second attack, police forces from both states increased patrols on the town's secluded back roads. A community that had once been friendly, where front doors were never locked and neighbors were always welcome, now grew eerily quiet after sundown.

Businesses saw a decline in customers, especially those catering to the night crowd. Residents were afraid to leave home, even during the daylight, for fear they may become the next target of the Phantom Killer. However, one industry in town became a hotspot for concerned citizens – the local hardware and ammo shops.

Residents bought up guns and ammo like crazy, hoping to be able to defend themselves from the attacks. Deadbolts and other home security devices became commonplace in all the towns households, and some homeowners were even seen setting up booby traps and other contraptions to catch the killer in his tracks.

Many of the town's local high school and college boys rounded up patrol groups. These men would go out at night with baseball bats and other makeshift weapons, hoping to catch the Phantom Killer on the prowl. None of them were ever successful.

Rumors continued to spread and impair the investigations. There was constant news about someone's son being arrested for the murders, or a suspect being charged, but these rumors rarely ever revealed themselves to be true. Police were forced to perform damage control on the stories spreading around town while also conducting their own investigation into the attacks.

Under the Spotlight

After the final attack, at the Starks farmhouse, authorities and media swarmed into Texarkana like never before. The quiet town was buzzing with news reporters from all across the nation, and reports of the murders were spreading to all areas of the country. Texarkana had never experienced the media's curious eye before.

The famous Texas Rangers stepped into the investigation, headed by the well-known Manuel "Lone Wolf" Gonzaullas. Gonzaullas was the first Ranger captain from Spanish descent, and was known for being a ruthless charmer in his day. He spent a great of his time providing interviews for national newspapers and radio broadcasts about the state of the investigation. He was even found one day taking pictures of the Starks crime scene with a young *Life* magazine reporter; neighbors had reported suspicious lights and sounds from the house when Gonzaullas and the woman were found.

While the local press, headed by the Texarkana Gazette, dubbed the suspected serial killer the "Phantom Killer" or "Phantom Slayer," national media clung to a different name: "The Moonlight Murderer." Because of this title, many believe that the murders were all committed under the full moon, when the nights were in fact at their darkest during the time of the crimes.

A Fruitless Investigation

The entire nation was on the lookout for a masked killer terrorizing young couples, with leads coming in from all areas of the South. In all, the authorities considered over four hundred separate suspects, but no one was ever charged with the attacks of that spring. While most of these suspects never received any public attention, the media caught wind of some of the more notable ones.

A middle-aged man from College Station, a Texas town several miles west of Texarkana, was at one point considered a prime suspect. He had previously been caught sneaking up on parked cars, typically with young couples inside, and brandishing a .22 rifle in order to threaten and rob them. While this man was never convicted of murder, many believed him to be the Phantom Killer based on the similar crime and weapon.

In Fayetteville, a young male graduate student of the University of Arkansas committed suicide. In the wake of his untimely death, a note was found containing a handwritten poem and confession to the murders in Texarkana. His military records showed he had showed "homosexual tendencies" during his time with the U.S. Navy, and at the time these tendencies were believed to be a mental disorder related to sexual crimes like rape or assault. Nothing of value ever came from this lead.

Several local residents accused an IRS agent of the crimes, seemingly because of his antisocial demeanor or because he had gotten on the town's bad side. Another man claimed to have committed the crimes during fits of amnesia. Neither of these claims resulted in an arrest.

In 1999 and 2000, several years after the last murder, an anonymous woman called surviving family members of the Phantom Killer's victims, claiming to be his daughter. She apologized for the actions of his crimes and begged for forgiveness from the families. There is speculation over whether these claims are valid, but many believe them to simply be a cry for attention. After all, the primary suspect of the Phantom Killer murders, Youell Swinney, never had a daughter.

Chasing a Criminal

During his time investigating the Moonlight Murders, Max Tackett, an Arkansas law officer, made a puzzling connection. Before each murder a car had been reported stolen and subsequently abandoned on the side of the rode. This information led police to believe that the Phantom Killer was using stolen vehicles to flee the crime scenes, and then dumping them before disappearing into the night.

The next car reported stolen triggered a police stakeout, with law enforcement hoping to find the killer connected to the vehicle. As police closed in on the stolen vehicle, Peggy Swinney was found to be driving. Police seized the car and took Peggy into custody, where she was questioned on how she came to possess the stolen vehicle.

Peggy revealed that Youell Swinney, a known car thief in Texarkana, had given the car to her, but that wasn't all she had to say. Peggy began telling police how Youell was the Phantom Killer, how he had assaulted and murdered all those couples, and how he had made her promise not to tell anyone. She included details of the crimes that had not been given to the public, information only known by police and the killer himself.

Before the police could move in on Youell Swinney, Peggy's story changed. She claimed that her previous confession was a lie, and that Youell was not the Phantom Killer after all. Eventually law enforcement discovered that Peggy and Youell had recently been married, making her unable to testify against her husband at all. While Youell remained an unofficial suspect, it seemed that the police were unable to touch him. But that changed in 1947, when Youell was arrested for auto theft.

At that time, Youell Swinney already had a long criminal record. He had been previously charged with counterfeiting, burglary, and assault, landing him in the Texas State Penitentiary for many years. After his release, he continued his work as a career criminal, but avoided capture for the time being.

During the investigation, police found evidence that Youell had owned a .32 Colt revolver, the murder weapon used to kill the second and third sets of victims, but that he had recently lost the gun in a failed card game. In hi home was also a shirt with the name "Stark" embroidered on the pocket, but it is unknown whether this shirt was actually connected to the Starks murder in the previous year.

With Youell in custody for auto theft, the police attempted to pin him as Texarkana's Phantom Killer. The man had a history of violence and sexual assault, and the record of stolen cars pointed toward his involvement in the murders. Youell never denied his innocence; he simply stayed quiet and refused to work with the police when questioned. A botched injection of "truth serum" during an interview in Little Rock, Arkansas, would eventually end the authorities' questioning of Youell regarding the Moonlight Murders. He was placed in prison for auto theft.

Youell remained in prison until 1973. Many of his cellmates recounted stories that Youell had told them, ones that included intimate details of the Phantom Killer's murder scenes and heavily suggested that Youell knew more than he let on. In 1994, Youell died a free man, never admitting to the Texarkana murders. To this day, most consider Swinney to be the Phantom Killer, even if he never served time for these crimes.

The Missing Woman

On June 1st, 1948, 21-year-old Virginia Carpenter departed Texarkana by train, on her way to her first semester of studying at the Texas State College for Women. She left Union Station at about 3PM, and headed for Denton, Texas and her new life as an educated woman. On the train ride, she met another student by the name of Marjorie Webster, who she shared a taxi with on the way to their dormitories.

Their taxi driver, Edgar Ray "Jack" Zachary, first dropped off Webster at the Fitzgerald dormitories, and then continued on to Brackenridge Hall, where Carpenter would be staying for the term. Zachary reported seeing Carpenter approach two young men in a yellow convertible outside the dorm, saying that she seemed to recognize them and was excited to see them. The next day, Zachary returned to the dorms to deliver some of Carpenter's luggage that she had forgotten at the station. He placed the trunk at the hall's front entrance and left, but no one ever claimed the luggage. That previous night would be the last time Virginia Carpenter was seen.

On June 4th, Carpenter's boyfriend, Kenny Branham, and her mother reported Virginia missing. After being brushed off by authorities, Mrs. Carpenter and other family members left for Denton late in the evening, hoping to help the police find Virginia.

Within several days, there were airplanes, motorboats, and on-foot search parties scanning the surrounding area for any sign of Virginia. Drivers of yellow convertibles were stopped and questioned, and Zachary was questioned by police and subjected to a polygraph test. Carpenter quickly became one of the most famous missing person cases in Texas, with her picture circulating across the country.

Before long, rumors started spreading back in Texarkana. Virginia Carpenter had personally known three of the Phantom Killer's victims, and some started to believe that she had a target on her back. Perhaps the killer had followed her from Texarkana to Denton, just another passenger on the crowded train. Or perhaps the killer was someone that Carpenter knew, like one of the men seen in the yellow convertible to night she went missing. Either way, many believe that this disappearance was connected to the attacks in 1946.

Countless sightings of Carpenter across Texas - riding in a car, buying groceries, or hitchhiking - continued to flow in, but no solid leads were ever discovered. By 1955, Carpenter was considered dead. She had been missing for seven years, and little hope remained of finding her. Despite this, tips continued to emerge on Carpenter's possible whereabouts.

In 1959, a wooden box was found buried with female remains inside that matched Carpenter's physical description. They were sent to Austin for examination, but the landowners soon confessed to digging them up from an old cemetery.

In 1998, a man called the police claiming to know where Carpenter's body was buried. He led police to the grounds of the Texas State College for Women, the school she was meant to attend, but the search came up empty.

Carpenter's disappearance causes some to doubt Youell Swinney's guilt. If her disappearance was a result of the Phantom Killer, the same man who brutally attacked at least three different couples, then this man could not be Swinney. At the time Carpenter went missing, Swinney was being held in prison for auto theft. Maybe Peggy Swinney had a hand in the disappearance of Carpenter, or her abduction was committed by someone other than the Phantom Killer, but it could not have been Swinney.

Phantoms Around the World

Some believe that the Phantom Killer simply moved his crimes to a new location, but it is likely he just inspired other killers to follow his pattern of attack. As the United States reached the height of violent crime and serial killers, attacks cropped up across the country and even abroad. The Phantom Kiiler's *modus operandi* (or M.O.) would become commonplace among serial killers in the coming decades, including the Zodiac Killer, Il Mostro, and the Son of Sam.

In 1946, a young couple was shot in Fort Lauderdale, Florida. Elaine Eldridge and Lawrence Hogan were parked outside Dania Beach when someone approached the vehicle and shot both victims with a .32 semi-automatic handgun. While the weapon used was not a Colt, it remained very similar to the one used in Texarkana. No fingerprints or footprints were found at the scene. With several similarities to the Texarkana attacks, many believed that the killer had relocated across the country. Texas, Arkansas, and Florida police worked together on the investigation, but no major connections were ever revealed to the public.

Located in San Francisco, the Zodiac Killer operated very similarly to the Phantom Killer during the late 1960s. He stalked young people in their vehicles and shot them with a revolver, and his identity remains unknown. However, unlike the Phantom Killer who personally avoided the media's attention, the Zodiac Killer was hungry for exposure. His main source of fame comes from sending cryptic notes to the Bay Area press, including four ciphers. Only one of these ciphers was ever solved, but it led the police no closer to identifying a suspect. These notes were examined top to bottom, in hopes of finding the true identity of the Zodiac Killer, but no leads were ever found.

Across the Atlantic Ocean, from 1968 to 1985, Florence, Italy was shook by sixteen murders. Dubbed Il Mostro or The Monster of Florence, the killer shot young couples parked alone in their cars with a .22 rifle. While four different suspects were arrested and charged with these murders throughout the years, the investigation has attracted scrutiny and many believe these men were actually innocent.

While the Son of Sam's identity is known today, his killings reflected those of the Phantom Killer and others. Operating in New York City in the mid 1970s, David Berkowitz killed six victims with a .44 Bulldog revolver. His attacks triggered the biggest manhunt in New York City, and for years women kept their hair short and avoided disco clubs for fear of being Berkowitz's next target. Like the Zodiac Killer, Berkowitz loved taunting the police and media with cryptic letters, where he promised to continue killing until he was caught. After his capture in 1977, Berkowitz enjoyed a bit of morbid celebrity for his crimes, which many reported he seemed to enjoy greatly. He remains in prison today, serving six life sentences.

While it is unlikely that the Phantom Killer actually relocated to be the Zodiac Killer or Il Mostro, some true crime experts believe it is possible. While the Phantom Killer was one of the first of his kind, looking back his killings were not exceptionally unique by today's standards.

It is easy to see how the Phantom Killer and his Moonlight Murders have shaped our ideas of killers today. Urban legends of a mad man stalking young couples in love, scratching on car doors and leaving bloody hooks behind, persist around campfires and in dark corners of the Internet. *The Town That Dreaded Sundown* might live among the likes of Freddy Krueger and Michael Myers, but it is a fictionalized retelling of the very real horrors that haunted Texarkana that year.

RAILROAD KILLER

They called him the 'Railroad Killer.'

Angel Resendiz earned the nickname because of his penchant for committing his crimes near railroads, using the rail cars as his own personal get-away system.

Committing murder after murder, he was able to elude both American and Mexican authorities for over a decade.

EARLY LIFE

A birth certificate found by the FBI listed his date of birth as August 1st, 1960. He was born To Virginia de Maturino in the town of Izucar de Matomoros in the state of Puebla, Mexico. His mother has stated adamantly that the correct spelling of his surname is Recendis not Resendiz although the killer would have over fifty different aliases throughout his lifetime.

Angel had spent his childhood years with relatives and not with his immediate family. According to his mother, he was sexually abused by an uncle and other pedophiles in the town of Puebla. He would spend his youth roaming the streets, robbing, stealing and sniffing glue. Relatives would later testify that Resendiz was routinely beaten as a child, one time being "jumped" by several other youths who beat him so bad that he bled through his ears. Resendiz would leave home for months at a time then suddenly return mumbling about a coming religious apocalypse.

Legal trouble came early for Resendiz as he was caught trying to sneak into the Texas border at the age of sixteen. This would become the first of numerous run-ins with border patrol agents until he finally made it into the United States, making his way to St. Louis and finding work with a manufacturing company under an assumed name. He even registered to vote with his false identification.

In September of 1979, at the age of nineteen, Resendiz was arrested for assault and car theft in Miami. He was tried and sentenced to twenty-years in prison but was released after only six years and sent back to Mexico.

But he wouldn't stay there for long.

Through numerous attempts of trial and error, Resendiz had learned not only to game the system but to enter and exit the United States with minimal detection.

He learn to use the rail-cars...

AN "INVISIBLE" MAN

Resendiz became so skilled at crossing the border without detection that he began charging for his services. He began to make a living as a human smuggler, transporting Mexicans across the border for a fee.

Resendiz soon developed a reputation for his smuggling skills, often being seen as a 'go to' person in his Ciudad Juarez neighborhood called 'Patria.'

He would make weekly crossings over the border, being arrested only intermittently. He would then be deported back into his native land only to ping-pong back and forth.

Finally, Resendiz would serve prison terms for his crimes. He would be arrested in Texas for false identity and citizenship, getting a year and half worth of jail.

Upon release in 1987, he journeyed to New Orleans and was arrested for carrying a concealed weapon. He received another year and half worth of prison time until parole.

He then went back to his old haunts in St. Louis where he tried to defraud Social Security and receive illegal payments. He got caught and served a three year sentence.

Resendiz then decided small-time burglaries were his deal. He once again illegally crossed the border, journeyed to New Mexico and was caught burglarizing a home. He was imprisoned for eighteen months and upon release he broke into a Santa Fe rail yard, being captured yet again.

"They should have called Resendiz the boomerang man," forensic psychologist Frank Lizzo said. "He knew how to play the game and seemingly had no fear of the system. The system never punished him severely enough for him to stop his crimes, let alone stop crossing the border."

After his last recorded deportation, the killings began.

THE KILLING FIELDS

"He probably started killing somewhere in his late 20s," Douglas said. "He may have killed people like himself initially – males, transients...(he) became angry at the population at large. What America represents here is this wealthy country where he keeps getting kicked out...(he) just can't make ends meet. Coupled with these feelings, these inadequacies, fueled by the fact that he's known to take alcohol, take drugs, lowers his inhibitions now to go out and kill."

Angel's list of victims began in 1986. Continuing to bounce in and out of the United States, he shot a homeless woman and left her for dead in an abandoned farm house. He had met the acquaintance of the woman at a homeless shelter and they became friends. They would later take a trip on a motorcycle together when he felt that the woman disrespected him.

Resendiz would then take out his gun and blow her head off.

The woman allegedly had a boyfriend whom Resendiz shot and killed as well. He said that he dumped his body in a creek between San Antonio and Uvalde. This killing has never been verified aside from what Resendiz revealed to the police during his interrogation sessions.

Five years later, Resendiz would kill Michael White because he was a "homosexual." Resendiz would bludgeon White to death with a brick and leave him in front of an abandoned home.

These were seemingly warm-ups for the more brutal crimes to come which would also include rape.

"Sex seemed almost secondary," FBI profiler John Douglas said when apprised of Resendiz's crimes. "(He is) just a bungling crook ...very disorganized."

Douglas would later concede, however, that it was this disorganization that worked in his favor. Like a true drifter, Resendiz' whereabouts became as elusive as a rational thought in his head.

"When he hitches a ride on the freight train, he doesn't necessarily know where the train is going," Douglas said. "But when he gets off, having background as a burglar, he's able to scope out the area, do a little surveillance, make sure he breaks into the right house where there won't be anyone to give him a run for his money. He can enter a home complete with cutting glass and reaching in and undoing the locks."

"He'll look through the windows and see who's occupying it. The guy's only 5 foot-7, very small. In fact...the early weapons were primarily blunt-force trauma weapons, weapons of opportunity found at the scenes. He has to case them out, make sure he can put himself in a win-win situation."

Resendiz would also leave his weapon of choice up to chance. Whatever the home would have, a statue a mantle piece, a butcher knife, that would become the instrument of murder.

FLORIDA KILLINGS

On March 23rd, 1997, Jesse Howell would be found bludgeoned to death beside the railroad tracks in Ocala, Florida. He was nineteen years old.

"When we got there," Sheriff Patty Lumpkin said. "We see what appears to be a young male, in his late teens or early twenties. Blood around the head area. You could tell by looking at him that he was dead. The first thing I do is make sure that we've got our forensics people on the way, on the medical examiners on the way, and all the investigators that we have called out or either there or en route."

"When those types of things happen it might have been someone who had fallen off a train," Lt. Jeff Owens said. "Or someone who could have been struck by a train."

The authorities quickly ruled out an accident, however, as they examined the body.

"It didn't appear to be an accident," Lumpkin said. "Because if he had been hit by the train the trauma would have been much more extreme. I've seen some deaths from trains and the initial impact from the train would have done more harm to the body."

The forensic team did determine that Howell's body looked as if he were the victim of blunt force trauma.

"We did see a baseball type of cap," forensic scientist Michael Dunn said. "It appeared to have blood on the inside surface of he bill. In addition, there was a pair of wire rimmed eye glasses and one of the eye pieces was missing, one of the lenses was out. This didn't look good either. As we moved closer, we saw that the victim had been dragged to that spot using just the blue jean material around the cuff (of his pants)."

Near the body, they found a brass and rubber coupling. This device was used to link one train car to another. It could also be used as a clubbing weapon.

"It had what appeared to be blood on it (the coupling)," Dunn recalled.

Howell still had jewelry on his person. He wore a gold cross necklace, a watch and a small amount of cash in his pocket. The police ruled out robbery as a motive.

The police did not identify Howell's body right off the bat. They did find a money wire receipt where some money had been wired from Illinois to Florida. The name on the receipt was of a woman named "Wendy."

Police tracked the money transfer to its point of origin which was all the way in Woodstock, Illinois.

Coincidentally, the authorities there were investigating the disappearance of Wendy Von Huben.

Wendy was missing alongside her boyfriend, the nineteen year old Jesse Howell.

"They advised me that they were investigating a John Doe," Woodstock Detective Kurt Rosenquest recalled. "Unidentified male."

Rosenquest then followed up with the investigating team in Florida, sending them the fingerprints and pictures of Jesse Howell.

The Ocala police would then positively identify Howell.

Jesse had met Wendy only months earlier. They had secretly planned to marry and went on a road trip with another couple.

The other couple, however, grew tired of Jesse and Wendy's constant bickering. They demanded to be let out of the car and left. Jesse and Wendy continued into Ocala, Florida where they ran out of money.

Wendy would call her parents in Illinois who would then transfer her $200 via Western Union. The couple would collect the $200 but would not return home.

"We checked Greyhounds," Rosenquest said. "Nobody matching their description ordered buses or train tickets back to the Woodstock area."

Tears were shed as Rosenquest informed Howell's parents that their teen son had been murdered. The investigative team then turned their attention to the disappearance of Wendy.

They held out hope because there were issues between her and Jesse, thinking that perhaps she simply ran off to be by herself.

Police scoured the surrounding areas and used helicopters in all directions around the railroad tracks.

They would find nothing. There was no DNA left behind on Jesse Howell's body either.

Papers and fliers with Wendy Von Huben's information was distributed all throughout Florida up through Illinois.

Authorities also began interviewing the transient population that lived along the railroad tracks.

Two and a half months later, however, Wendy's parents would receive a phone call.

"The phone rang," Rosenquest recalled. "Wendy's father answered the phone. The girl was crying. She said 'I'm sorry. I love you.'"

She would tell the father she was two hours away from Woodstock at a gas station. The father asked for the phone number on the pay phone she was calling from and she said that there wasn't any before hanging up.

The police were not certain that the phone call came from Wendy so they immediately headed out to the gas station where they believe the call took place.

Police tracked down the surveillance video of the gas station. On the video, a woman that physically resembled Wendy entered the gas station.

The phone records, however, revealed that the call did not come from the gas station where the surveillance video revealed a woman who allegedly was Wendy. It came from another gas station where there were fliers posted of Wendy.

Someone had played a cruel hoax as Wendy's parents had added their home number to the fliers

ONE-LEGGED BOB AND A CHANCE DISCOVERY

A year went by without any sign of Wendy.

There was some ray of hope, however, as the railroad authorities called the Ocala police and informed them that the received information from a member of one of the homeless camps. They had a man in custody named "One Legged Bob" who was traveling with a girl and may be responsible for the murder of her previous boyfriend.

"'One Legged Bob' was your typical homeless person," Owens said. "Kinda scruffy. Hadn't shaved in a few days. He had a prosthetic leg that helped him get around. For someone who you might consider crippled, he was far from crippled."

Owens would spend the next eight hours interviewing the only lead he had, a one legged homeless man.

After the grueling interrogation, Owens realized that he had the wrong suspect.

By sheer chance, however, Patty Lumpkin heard about someone they dubbed the "Railroad Killer" during a class she was taking at the FBI.

"They called him the Railway Killer," Lumpkin recalled. "The Angel of Death. He was killing people. Leaving them near the railroad or he was killing them at homes or locations that were close to the railroad.

The FBI knew the Railway Killer as Angel Resendiz.

"We knew that Angel Resendiz was a person that rode the rails across the country," FBI Agent Mark Young said. "We were worried where he'd wind up next. So we decided to make him a top ten fugitive. Maybe the millions of eyes of the public would tell us something."

The strategy worked.

"He was one of the most vile, evil persons that I had ever dealt with," Young said. "It was like every time you turn around there's another murder."

Owens and Lumpkin hoped to talk to Resendiz to query him about Jesse Howell's murder and Wendy Von Huben's disappearance.

"The attorneys representing him at the time in Texas stopped us," Owens said. "They wanted to protect their client from talking. Any defense attorney who represents a criminal will generally tell the person to stop talking to law enforcement."

Resendiz was placed on death row and Texas had a fast execution rate. The two detectives worried that they would lose their chance to interview Resendiz and connect him to the crimes in Ocala.

Owens and Lumpkin decided to mail Resendiz a letter, respectfully asking him if they could interview him. The letter was written in a formal manner and even addressed him as "Senor."

To their surprise, Resendiz responded back and granted them an interview regarding his involvement in Jesse's killing and Wendy's disappearance.

During their meeting, Resendiz was quick to admit that he had killed Jesse. The detectives deliberately withheld information about the killing, holding back details that only the killer would know. But when Resendiz described using a brake coupling from one of the trains, they knew they had their killer.

But they needed to find out what happened to Wendy.

In a follow-up letter, they promised him immunity from prosecution if he agreed to talk. It was a moot point by then as he was already on death row but the detectives still needed permission from Wendy's family to go through with the interview.

In order to receive some sense of closure, the family agreed to the immunity.

"When we get to the prison," Lumpkin said. "We see him coming down the hallway. He (Resendiz) has a waist belt on. It's an electric shock belt and he's chained to the belt. He's just a mild-mannered person but remember that a psychopath or a sociopath doesn't have any feeling. I mean he had dead eyes. He had no feeling in that body. He didn't care about anything."

Resendiz would reveal that he was heading south for work when the train stopped and he spotted Jesse getting off the train for a smoke.

"Resendiz told us that he killed Jesse with a piece of the train coupling," Lumpkin said. "And Wendy was asleep on the train when this took place. And then when they went down the road further somehow he talked Wendy into getting off the train."

Resendiz then raped and strangled Wendy to death.

Resendiz drew a map of where had left Wendy's body. He described burying her in a shallow grave near a canopy of trees. Resendiz would remember that she had a book in a back pack and an army style jacket that he used to cover her fresh grave.

Police would return to the site and were able to locate where he buried Wendy's body. Almost three years after the murder, everything the killer described was still there. The book. The jacket.

And Wendy's body.

"When Wendy ran away she had a small engagement ring," Owen said. "And she had a Winnie the Pooh wristwatch."

The detective would bring those items back to Wendy's parents.

KENTUCKY RAILROAD MURDER

In August of 1997, Resendiz would make his way from Ocala, Florida to Lexington, Kentucky. It was there he would stalk two young college students.

Holly Dunn was a 20-year old junior at the University of Kentucky and it was there she met Christopher Maier.

"Chris Maier was my very good friend," Dunn recalled. "He was just the nicest, kindest man. We decided that we wanted to be more than friends then we started dating. We dated for about three months."

"Chris and I were attending a party. We decided that the party wasn't very fun so we went to go talk a walk by the railroad tracks. We sat down and talked for awhile and when we got up to leave a man came out from behind an electrical box. He had a weapon that he used on Chris. It was some sort of ice pick or screw driver. Something sharp. I guess our immediate thought was he's going to rob us. That's when we realize he wants money we start thinking 'okay, well, you could have our credit card, you can have our ATM card, you can have our car.' Then he started tying up Chris' hands behind his back. And then he came over to me and he took off my belt and that's when I started thinking he doesn't want to rob us."

After tying up Holly, Resendiz then pulled Chris by the shirt across the railroad tracks and into a ditch.

Holly would follow on her knees, pleading for him to stop whatever he was about to do.

"Lie down," Resendiz said, his voice soft but menacing.

"Everything is going to be okay," Christopher said to Holly as Resendiz dragged him into the ditch.

"Shut up!" Resendiz commanded as he gagged Christopher with a sock.

Resendiz then walked off into the darkness. The frightened couple did not know what the psychopath had planned.

"Then he comes with this rock," Holly recalled. "There was no warning, he drops this rock on Chris' head. I'm just thinking 'what just happened?' I don't even know what just happened."

"You don't have to worry about him anymore," Resendiz said to Holly as he got on top of her.

"I went into survival mode, I'm thinking, I mean he's gonna kill me. I may as well fight. I'm gonna fight. He unties my feet and climbs on top of me. I start to kick and scream and hit him but he held that knife or ice pick (to my throat) and said 'look how easily I could kill you.' I stopped everything and then he raped me."

"I memorized his face," Dunn said. "I stared at him and memorized, he had a tattoo on his arm, I was thinking if you have any scars I'm gonna remember your scars, I'm gonna remember your face, I'm not gonna forget it because if I live through this I will get you."

Resendiz completed the sexual assault of Dunn before smashing her head with a rock.

"He hit me five or six times in my face," Dunn recalled. "I think I put my hand up and then I turned over and then he hit me five or six times in the back of my head. He hit me hard. He was trying to kill me. I think I laid there and he thought I was dead."

Resendiz did think she was did as he threw the rock down and ran away from the crime scene.

Holly would suffer severe facial trauma but miraculously survived the attack.

"I had a broken jaw," Dunn said. "Broken eye socket and cuts on the back of my head that they had to staple shut and then I had cuts on my face."

She woke up in a Kentucky hospital, surrounded by family members.

"Everyone was told not to talk about Chris to me. I just said 'Chris is dead, isn't he?' And my Dad actually is the one I said that to and he was like 'yes, he died.'"

TEXAS TERROR

Resendiz would travel to Texas via train and in October of 1988 he flopped down in Hughes Springs. He would enter the home of 87-year old Leafie Mason, attacking the woman with an iron and killing her.

Two months later, Resendiz would sneak into the home of Dr. Claudia Benton, a thirty-nine year old medical researcher who lived in a suburb of Houston near the railroad tracks.

Again, it was a case of a home being to close to the train tracks. The train would provide the perfect cover for the sneaky Resendiz as he realized that the sound of the rail-car racing by would allow him to break in homes without being heard.

He applied the same technique with Benton, breaking into her home, raping then killing her.

Police would find the doctor face down on the floor. Her bedroom soaked in blood, ransacked for any valuables.

He head had been covered in a plastic bag while her body had been covered in a blanket.

"It appears that she (Claudia Benton) was sleeping," recalled Ken Macha, former police sergeant. "He was able to get in and picked up a bronze statuette from the mantle in the living room. He was relentless in beating her. The skull fractures themselves would have been enough to kill her. She was then stabbed in the back with a very large butcher knife."

"Resendiz was brutal, sadistic," said former West University police chief Gary Brye.

Fingerprints and DNA evidence would link Resendiz to the crime.

The problem was they could catch the man that Texas Ranger Drew Carter referred to as "a walking, breathing form of evil."

EVADING POLICE

Seven months later, Resendiz would continue to avoid capture. He remained in Texas, riding the rail cars until coming into the town of Weimar. He would break into the home of Pastor Norman "Skip" Sirnic and his wife Karen. Resendiz smashed a jack hammer into both of their heads, killing them instantly. He would then rape the body of Karen postmortem.

"He would watch these places," prosecuting attorney Devin Anderson said. "He would watch them, wait for them to go to sleep, get in their house and he would strike them before they would even wake up. I thought we have got to catch this guy."

The DNA found at the scene of the Sirnic murders would match those left on Benton. The FBI then realized they had a highly mobile serial killer on the loose...someone who could kill in one town then appear in another town miles away and kill again.

Resendiz was also smart. He would constantly alter his appearance. He'd shave his head. Then his mustache. He'd be clean shaven one week. Unkempt the next. He would wear glasses one week. No glasses the next.

Authorities could not get an accurate description of him other than the fact that he was small.

Resendiz was also able to take advantage of the lack of a coordinated computer system that gave law enforcement the ability to cross-check fugitives. After the Sirnic murders, Border Patrol had encountered Resendiz near the El Paso border but did not find him on the wanted list.

They then deported him back to Mexico.

Within 48 hours, Resendiz was back across the border to resume his killing spree.

"Our computers told us that he was nothing of lookout material," said C.G. Almengor, a supervisor at the border."We really wish he had been in the system so we could have caught him."

Resendiz would be deported no less than seventeen times over the course of his rampage. At no point did authorities make the connection because of his changing appearance, use of different aliases and the lack of a connected system to document illegals trying to come across the border.

A PREFERENCE FOR TEXAS

Noemi Dominguez was a graduate of Rice University who had just recently quit her job as an elementary school teacher to pursue a master's degree.

She was described as "the sweetest, nicest teacher – a darling who went the extra mile."

Fueled by hate, Resendiz would break into Noemi's home and rape her before killing her with a pick ax. He then stole her car and drove to Schulenberg, Texas where he would kill Josephine Konvicka with the same pick ax.

He would leave the weapon embedded in Konvicka's head as well as leave his fingerprints all over the home. He was more than just sloppy, he was getting cocky. He left a newspaper article that described his crimes as well as a toy train...a reference to his nickname as the "Railroad Killer."

Resendiz was also meticulous in approaching his victims.

"He undid the light in her (Noemi's) car," Anderson said. "So when he opened the door it wouldn't come on. That's who were were dealing with. Someone who really knew how to sneak around. Who really knew how to avoid detection."

"He kept killing people. He would not stop. In his mode of transportation, using the railroads was brilliant because they couldn't be monitored. I mean there's thousands of trains and millions of miles of tracks all over the United States."

"I felt hopeless at the time. Because if you're willing to sleep in a train or you're willing to sleep in a field, you can stay lost for a long, long time and I didn't think we were ever going to catch him."

Later that month, Resendiz had journeyed to Illinois, reaching the town of Gorham. He would break into the home of 80-year old George Morber and his daughter Carolyn Frederick. Resendiz would tie Morber to a chair and shoot him in the back of the head with a shotgun. He then raped Carolyn and smashed the shotgun across her head with such force that the weapon broke in half.

Both Morber and Frederick would die from their injuries.

The FBI placed him on their Top Ten list.

They then recruited his common-law wife, Julietta Reyes, and brought her into Houston for questioning from her hometown of Rodeo, Mexico.

Reyes complied with police requests, turning over over ninety-three pieces of jewelry that her husband had mailed to her from the U.S.

Relatives of Noemi Dominguez claimed thirteen pieces. George Benton was able to identify some pieces of jewelry as belonging to his wife as well.

Police would then locate Resendiz's half-sister, Manuela Karkiewicz, who lived in New Mexico. Initially, she refused to cooperate. She worried that the FBI or the police would kill her brother. But Carter convinced her to talk Resendiz into giving himself up.

The FBI knew that Resendiz had made his way back to Mexico after the murders in Illinois and was hiding in his hometown neighborhood of Patria.

Carter was able to get a rapport with Manuela. He convinced her that Resendiz would receive "personal safety while in jail, regular visiting rights for his family and a psychological evaluation."

"I came away with the impression that they (Resendiz' family) definitely had an understanding of right and wrong ... and knew now that what Maturino Resendiz was accused of doing was heinous and wrong ... ," Carter said. "Manuela, especially, came across as a woman of strong faith. There was a very deep emotional strain and burden placed on her in this investigation. She had to make some very difficult choices that impacted her and her family. And, in the end, her actions alone speak to her character."

Carter spent weeks talking to Manuela who in turn "worked a miracle."

They got the serial killer to surrender.

On July 12th, Manuela would receive a fax from the district attorney's office in Harris County which formalized everything that Texas Ranger Carter had promised.

The word passed from Manuela to another relative who acted as a go-between with Resendiz. The relative than came back later that evening and said that Resendiz would surrender in the morning at 9 a.m.

Texas Ranger Drew Carter would accompany Manuela and a spiritual adviser to meet with Resendiz on a bridge that connected El Paso, Texas to Ciudad Juarez.

"When I saw that face there was a little bit of excitement there because I finally said, 'This is going to happen,'" Carter recalled as he remembered Resendiz appearing on the bridge with his dirty jeans, muddy boots and blank facial expression. "He stuck out his hand, I stuck out my hand, and we shook hands."

Resendiz would then surrender to the Texas Ranger.
DEATH PENALTY

Resendiz' attorneys knew that their only hope would be an insanity defense. The Mexican government also got involved, lobbying authorities to spare Resendiz the death penalty

"Insanity was the logical defense because no one wants to believe that there is someone out there who would do things like that," Anderson said. "That was the thing that worried me the most about the case was that jurors would just throw up their hands and say nobody in their right mind could do what he does."

"The thing about what a life sentence with Resendiz would have been, he would have enjoyed it. I mean he would have had pen pals. He would have given interviews if they let him, I mean he would have loved it. And I knew that. And he didn't deserve to live after what he did just didn't. He caused so much pain, so much heartache and so much terror, that's what the whole focus of the trial had to be."

George Benton, the husband of Claudia, would vehemently criticize the Mexican government who support his appeals and domestic opposition to the death penalty.

"(He)looked like a man and walked like a man. But what lived within that skin was not a human being."

"He was small," Anderson said when she first saw Resendiz in the courtroom. "Maybe five- foot five. His forearms though, were roped with muscles. He was scary. Even though he was small you could feel he was dangerous. He looked like a wild animal who'd been caught."

Resendiz looked "timid" in the courtroom and spoke of himself in religious riddles. He claimed he was Jewish and didn't seem effected when he was informed that the prosecution was aiming for the death penalty.

"I don't believe in death," Resendiz, said. "I know the body is going to go to waste. But me, as a person, I'm eternal. I'm going to be alive forever."

The defense said that Resendiz' crimes were caused by head injuries, drug abuse and a family history of mental illness. He has a delusional perception of the world as he believes that he can cause earthquakes, floods, and explosions and that God told him to kill his victims whom they believed to be evil.

He made a living stealing things from his victims and having his wife sell them in Mexico. "That was his job," Anderson said. "And for recreation it was killing the people who lived in the house."

"He was a very intelligent person who worked the system and knew exactly what kinds of things to say to get that defense to work."

The jury, however, would find Resendiz guilty after one hour and forty-five minutes of deliberation.

He was sentenced to die via lethal injection.

"He made it very clear during my conversation with him that he deserves to die," Owens said.

"I want to ask if it is in your heart to forgive me," Resendiz said in his final words. "You don't have to. I know I allowed the devil to rule my life. I just ask you to forgive me and ask the Lord to forgive me for allowing the devil to deceive me. I thank God for having patience with me. I don't deserve to cause you pain. You did not deserve this. I deserve what I am getting."

Resendiz then prayed in Hebrew and Spanish before drawing his final breath.

House of Horror : The True Story of Rosemary West

Mary Gilmore

Unfortunately, it's not unusual in this day and time to turn on the news and hear a warning about a new serial killer roaming our streets. It's horrifying and hard to comprehend what could possibly make a person commit such heinous crimes. What is wrong with this person that drives him or her to commit such an act? The truth is that people have searched for the answers to that question for a very long time. Unfortunately, it still remains a mystery for the most part.

Rosemary West is one of those baffling cases. We will look deeper into her life and learn how her inner demons progressed to becoming one of Britain's most notorious and sadistic serial killers, taking the lives of at least 10 young women and girls.

Most of the information obtained by the authorities came from her husband and partner in crime, victims who escaped or were permitted to leave, and a great deal from her own children. Rosemary has offered very limited insight into the story, even to this day.

Remarkably, she did not act alone in committing these grisly deeds. This story is immensely complex, which I will attempt to sort out and then tie it all together with the union of Rose Letts West and Fred West in their vicious killing spree. There will be accounts of child abuse, rape, sexual deviance, torture, and murder. Rosemary West's crimes were so horrendous; it may be difficult for some of you to read.

Rosemary West's Early Life

Rosemary's mother came into her room one morning to wake her for school. Rosemary probably knew by the familiar expression on her mother's face that this would be one of those mornings that fills her life with constant dread. As she gets dressed, she begins preparing herself for what she knows is probably about to occur.

As she walks into the kitchen, breakfast is the last thing on her mind. Instead, she braces herself for the punishment she is about to receive. Don't misunderstand, Rosemary hadn't done anything wrong, but her father didn't need a reason.

His kind of punishment wasn't a time-out or a swat on the behind as most children receive. His were the kind that affect a child for a lifetime. Rose has no idea whether she is about to be beaten or if she'll endure other horrors that her father is known to inflict.

That is a likely scenario in the life of Rosemary West. Her father was a paranoid schizophrenic. The mental illness along with other problems, made life for her, her mother, and her siblings a nightmare. The abuse was bad enough, but what made it even more terrifying was not knowing from one minute to the next when or why her father's rage would erupt.

As a result of her home life, Rose made bad grades and became overweight. To make her situation worse, she was teased and bullied at school, giving her no relief from the continuous damage to her self-esteem.

There's a possibility that Rosemary's destiny was sealed much earlier in her life. It's not surprising that Rosemary's mother suffered from severe depression. The illness was so debilitating that she received electroconvulsive therapy several times while Rosemary was still in the womb, one of which occurred just before Rosemary's birth. There were some that thought this therapy was the reason for Rosemary's frequent outbursts of anger as well as her inability to do well in school.

Most of us would be unable to imagine a childhood such as the one led by Rosemary West.

Why do They Kill?

There are no exact traits of a serial killer to help us understand what drives them to kill. Some of them come from a two parent loving home while others have divorced parents. Some had abusive parents and others had loving parents.

Some think it's due to a head or brain injury sometime in their life; however, most people that have had brain injuries do not become killers. The majority of serial killers are men who act alone. Rosemary is not only a woman, she also had a partner in her life of crimes. Female killers and couples represent only a small percentage of serial killings.

The Federal Bureau of Investigation did a symposium, which was comprised of 135 experts who have dealt with serial killers in various ways to determine commonalities of serial killings. They determined that there are no definitive common traits. However, the central nervous system is constantly developing in adolescence, which determines a person's social coping system. That is, they develop the way they interact with their peers such as in negotiation and compromise. If it does not develop adequately, it can result in violent behavior.

It would be safe to say that the events of Rosemary West's childhood could be a factor in the choices she made later in life.

Rosemary's Life Before the Murders

Rosemary Letts was the fifth child born to Bill and Daisy Letts in Devon, England on the 29th of November in 1953. She normally went by the shorter version of her name, Rose. As we've seen, Rose's childhood was unlike most other children's. In pictures of Rose at a younger age she had an ever present smile on her face. You wouldn't guess that she was going through hell within the walls of her home.

The Letts family lived in Northam, a charming seaside town in Devon. Neighbors thought of Bill Letts as a nice man; however, they must have thought it strange that they rarely saw his children. When they did, the children were mainly seen walking around in their garden. One neighbor stated that they really didn't seem to be playing at all. They were just walking around and rarely seen outside the walls of the garden.

What they didn't know was that the children weren't allowed outside the walls and were afraid to play because they were forbidden to get dirty.

Although Rose's father constantly punished the children including Rose, he was not as physically abusive with Rose as with his wife and the other children. It was thought that he didn't physically abuse her as much as the others because he thought there was something not quite right about her.

Some people thought that he didn't hurt Rose as much because he was using her for his sexual pleasures instead. Others speculated that Rose learned at a very young age that she could control her father's anger by using sex.

Rose's mother Daisy, eventually left her father. She moved out of their house taking Rose and the other children with her, freeing them from the abusive environment. Remarkably, after a brief time, Rose moved back in with her father who resumed sexually abusing her.

One day, as Rose waited for a bus, she was approached by a man. Rose described him as a dirty man who had disgusting green teeth. She and the man struck up a conversation and even though his appearance was repulsive by most people's standards, Rose became attracted to him. The man's name was Fred West.

West was raising his daughter and stepdaughter at that time so Rose began babysitting the two girls. In addition, Rose and Fred also became a couple.

Fred's Early Years

Fred West, the son of Walter and Daisy West, was born in Much Marcle, England in 1941. He was the second of their six children. Growing up, he was considered to be a nice boy. They appeared to be a normal family, however, Fred's upbringing was perhaps even worse than Rosemary's. According to Fred, the motto around his house by his father was, "Do whatever you want, just don't get caught."

Fred would later reveal to police that incest was a common occurrence in his household. He said his father regularly had sex with his own daughters. Fred also claimed that his father introduced him to bestiality. In addition, it was thought that his mother Daisy took his virginity when he was 12-years-old.

Not surprising, Fred did not do well in school and dropped out at the age of 15. Two years later, he was involved in a tragic motorcycle accident. He received a broken arm and leg and a fractured skull. The head injury put him in a coma for eight days. Afterward, his family claimed that thereafter, he frequently become enraged without warning. Amazingly, two years later, he received another head injury. In this instance, he fell from a fire escape causing unconsciousness for 24 hours.

Fred's history of child abuse and head injuries would certainly coincide with the conceivable characteristics of a serial killer.

At the age of 20, he was caught and arrested for molesting a 13-year-old girl who subsequently became pregnant. He was convicted, but for unknown reasons he was not sentenced to prison. The reason is possibly because the girl's parents and Fred's parents were friends. Even with his family's propensity for deviant sexual acts, they had recently decided to try their hand at getting religion, therefore, they disowned Fred after this latest incident.

Fred had problems keeping a normal job. He landed a construction job; however, he was caught stealing. In addition, he continued to get caught molesting more young girls. It's amazing how he could still be roaming the streets even back at that point.

Shortly after, when West was around 21, he ran into a former girlfriend named Catherine Costello. She was better known as Rena, which was the name she used while prostituting and the name stuck. In addition, Rena was an accomplished thief. Nevertheless, even with her reputation, she was described by neighbors and other acquaintances as a very nice person and an exceptionally good mother.

Even though she was already pregnant with another man's child at the time, things heated up between her and Fred again and they married about two months later. The baby girl was born in February

1963 and was named Charmaine. Rena had another child by Fred a year later and named her Anna Marie. You will hear the names of these two girls in a shocking context later in the story.

Unbelievably, someone gave Fred West a job driving an ice cream van. This wouldn't seem a proper job for Fred the child molester to say the least. For Fred, it was the perfect job with young girls running after him. It was an ideal way for him to find victims.

While working at this job, a four-year-old boy ran into the street in front of his van and the child was killed. After this incident, even though the death was accidental, Fred feared people in the area would seek retribution for the boy's death. He thought it would be in his best interest to move away.

At the time, a woman named Isa McNeil was caring for the West's children. Additionally, Rena had become friends with a young woman named Anne McFall. They all moved with Fred to *The Lakeside* caravan park in Bishop's Cleeve, Gloucestershire, which is where Fred would later live with Rose.

With Fred's sadistic habits still intact, there were soon problems in this odd household. Fred insistently pushed his warped sexual necessities onto all three women. It became too much for his wife, Rena, and the children's nanny, McNeil, so the two of them moved to Scotland. On the other hand, the other woman, Ann McFall, had warmed up to Fred and stayed behind. Besides, she had already become impregnated by him.

Fearful of Fred, Rena and Isa's planned was to keep their departure secret from him and sneak away. Unfortunately, McFall told Fred, which enraged him. He allowed them to leave, but not with the two children, so the two women fled to Scotland. Rena returned frequently to visit her children.

After that, McFall began to pressure Fred to divorce Rena and marry her. Apparently, this didn't set well with Fred. When she was eight months pregnant with Fred's child, she completely vanished. She was never reported missing, but her body was later discovered in a field minus her fingers and toes, which had been removed and were missing.

Fred was left to care for his daughter and stepdaughter.

The Evil Duo Unites

Around this time is when Fred met Rose at the bus stop. It was at the time when Fred was caring for his step-daughter and biological daughter, so Fred already had at least the one murder of Anne McFall under his belt when he met Rose. Rose then began taking care of the two children.

When they first got together Rose was only 16-years-old and Fred was 12 years older at 28. Her father absolutely disapproved of the relationship. He threatened West that if he didn't leave Rose alone he would call Social Services due to Rose's young age. That was ironic since her father had been having sex with her himself for a long time. Of course, that was most likely the reason he didn't want her to go.

Nevertheless, Rose moved in with Fred and they lived together as a family with Fred's two daughters. After only about two months, they married she moved in with him at *The Lakeside Caravan Park* in Bishop's Cleeve, Gloucestershire, where Fred had lived with Rena and Anne.

Of course Fred, a man of few scruples, soon introduced his young and damaged wife to a sadistic world of pornography and urged her into prostitution. Due to Rose's demoralizing childhood, it didn't take a lot of urging for her to become caught up in his world.

Not one to hold down a regular job, Fred's contribution to the income was mainly by thievery. He wasn't very accomplished at that either and was frequently caught and arrested. It wasn't long before he was sent to prison for 10 months, leaving young Rose in charge of his two daughters.

To make matters worse, she had become pregnant and gave birth to her daughter, Heather, in 1970 while Fred was still in jail. Being young in addition to having mental problems, caring for three children was a tall order for Rose and she didn't handle the situation well, to say the least.

To add to the pressure, seven-year-old Charmaine, began to be unruly and Rose was unable to cope with it. Years later, according to the other child, Anna Marie, it was not unusual for both girls to receive severe beatings; however, no matter how bad the beating, Charmaine refused to cry. This infuriated Rose so it's no surprise that Charmaine didn't seem to be around any longer after that.

This is thought to be when Rose committed her first murder. Rose's tendency to lose her temper most likely caused her to loss control and kill Charmaine. Apparently, Rose hid the girl's body, because it's known that Fred disposed of the body after he returned from prison.

Fred would hold this over Rose in the future. On one of the occasions when Rose's father tried to convince her to leave Fred and come home, Fred made a remark that was something like, "Come on now Rose, you know what we have between us." For someone that didn't know Fred, it would sound like an expression of love. More than likely with Fred, it was his not so subtle way of saying, "You can't leave. I have too much on you." She later told her parents that Fred would do anything, including murder.

Fred's first undertaking after returning from jail was to dismembered and dispose of Charmaine's body. For whatever sick reason, as with Anne McFall, he removed her fingers and toes and then buried her. This became the normal process in Fred's body disposal. It was later speculated that Fred and Rose were possibly involved in Satan worship. It is thought by some that removing the fingers and toes of their sacrifices was typical for Satan worshipers.

The next time Rena Costello came to visit her daughter it naturally created a problem when she discovered her daughter's absence, thanks to Rose. As you can imagine, Rena was not happy about her missing daughter and demanded some answers. Therefore, Rose and Fred must have decided that Rena would have to go as well. So this visit to see her little girl resulted in Rena's demise as well. Minus her fingers and toes, she was buried in a field close to the Caravan Hotel where Rose and Fred still lived.

That meant a total of at least three people had already lost their lives courtesy of Fred and Rose West. One each for Rose and Fred and now Rena by both of them.

A brief time later, Rose gave birth to their second child, Mae. They bought a large two-story house in Gloucester; however, there was not much money coming in. Fred started putting up panels in the rooms to create multiple bedrooms called bedsits. They were tiny rooms, which didn't fit much more than a bed. They began renting out these rooms for extra income; however, the rooms served another purpose as well.

By this time, Rose's fulltime career had become *prostitute*. They also began working other women out of the house. One of the rooms labeled "Rose's Room" was dedicated to Rose for turning tricks. Outside the door was a red light, which was lit when the room was in business. The children knew they were not to disturb when the red light was on. The room also came complete with a peephole, which was Fred's method for watching his wife in action and for making videos.

Both Rose and Fred had come from a family where incest was normal. It was not unnatural to them when Rose's own father occasionally came to their house to have sex with her.

In around October of 1972, Rose and Fred hired Carol Owens as a new nanny for their children. She told her story years later stating that Fred and Rose attempted to bring her into their twisted lifestyle. Not wanting any part of it, she soon left their house.

A few weeks later, as she was walking home, Fred pulled up beside her and offered a ride. The next thing she knew he hit her on the head. When she awoke, her hands were tied and Fred was in the process of taping her mouth.

She was told that if she tried to resist, Fred would call in his friends and let them have their way with her and she would then be killed.

They said they would bury her under the paving stones outside their home along with hundreds of other girls. Terrified, she didn't attempt to resist.

Unbelievably, they allowed her to leave the next day and she proceeded to file charges on them. Fred somehow managed to convince the court that the sex was consensual. In addition, Owens decided that testifying against these two could be an unhealthy choice.

The couple was given a meager fine on a charge of indecent assault and then released. She would be the last victim that the Wests' would allow to leave alive.

Years later, she regretted not testifying. She felt that if she had, it could have saved the lives of numerous women and girls and she was most likely correct.

One day, Fred and Rose arrived home and their neighbor, Elizabeth Agius, was outside. She had become friendly with the couple, so Fred stopped for a chat. Just in conversation, she asked what they had been doing, so Fred proceeded to tell her exactly what they had been up to.

He said they were cruising around looking for young girls. He must have felt he needed to explain why his wife would go along with him on such an outing. He said they figured the girls would see Rose and wouldn't be scared to get in the car. She would later say that she thought he must be joking...he wasn't.

Meanwhile, Fred was busy redecorating the cellar. One of the prostitutes that worked in the house later told authorities that she saw black suits, masks, chains, and whips down there. Fred had created his own torture chamber.

Anna Marie, Fred's remaining child with Rena Costello, was the first to be brutalized in Fred's torture chamber. She was bound, gagged, and violently raped as Rose watched. She was only eight-years-old at the time and this treatment would continue for years.

Eventually, Anna Marie moved out of the house to live with her boyfriend, which quite possibly saved her life. Again, letting her go would prove to be a bad move for the Wests later in court. As one of the survivors, a considerable amount of the horror stories came from her.

After Anna Marie's departure, Fred's attentions naturally turned to his daughters Heather and Mae; however, Heather wanted no part of it and resisted. Understandably, she was unable to keep it to herself and told a friend about the horrors happening at home. This would seal her fate, but Fred later claimed to police that her death was accidental.

The life of Rose and Fred West continued filled with the unimaginable. They would go on to have a total of seven children who were born in a short time span. It is believed that three are by Fred, one is by her own father, and the remaining three are from her clients. It almost seemed that their reason for having children was so Fred and Rose would have someone to torture at the times when no one else was tied up in the cellar. You can certainly say with certainty that Fred and Rose West were definitely not loving parents.

The One's That Didn't Survive the Terror

Over the next few years, the abuse of the West's children continued as did the murders of others. At some point, Fred went to work at a slaughter house. It was thought that this is when his already violent habits became even more gruesome. It could have been a factor in his fascination for dismembering his victims.

It is believed the next victim was Lynda Gough who was a personal acquaintance of the West's. She enjoyed participating in some of their sexual activities by sharing sex partners with Rose. However, for unknown reasons she later vanished. Gough's mother came to the West's house looking her daughter and was told that she moved in order to pursue a job. While she was speaking to the woman, Rose was wearing some of Linda Gough's clothing.

Carol Ann Cooper, only 15-years-old, is thought to be the next victim. She disappeared while walking home from the movies.

Evidence showed she died by strangulation, was dismembered, and buried in the garden.

Lucy Partington was in town visiting her family and a friend over the Christmas holidays. She went to the bus station to take a bus back home and most likely Fred, being one to hang out at bus stations asked her if she wanted a ride. As Fred and Rose planned, it is thought that the only reason she let them even approached her was due to the presence of Rose.

It is thought that they kept Partington in captivity for about a week after she vanished because poor Fred showed up at the hospital about a week later with a large laceration needing stitches. Authorities think he received the cut while cutting up Partington.

Shirley Hubbard went missing when she was returning home from Droitwich. There was definitive evidence of her torture. Her head was completely wrapped with tape with only a short rubber tube in her mouth to breath.

Juanita Marian Mott was a former tenant of the Wests'. Her torture was obvious. She was gagged with a binding made of socks, tights, and a bra, which were all stuffed inside each other. She was also tied up with clothes line rope looped around her thighs, arms, wrists, and ankles. This was done with the rope going back and forth around her horizontally and vertically until she was completely immobilized. She also had a rope with a noose, which most likely suspended her from the rafters in the cellar.

Shirley Anne Robinson was one of the prostitutes that worked out of their house who had sexual relations with both Fred and Rose. She became pregnant by Fred, at the same time Rose was pregnant by one of her clients.

Shirley began to get the idea she would like to replace Rose, which is not advisable in this family. Rose demanded that she had to go. She and her unborn child were dismembered and buried in the back garden. The cellar was full of bodies by this time and the back garden became the new burial grounds.

Therese Siegenthaler was a hitchhiker in route from London to Ireland. Some of the evidence showed that like Partington, she was kept alive for close to a week during which time she was likely tortured and raped.

Allison Chambers was the last known non-related victim. She was killed in 1979.

Their oldest daughter, Heather Ann West, was the last known victim. Fred claims he killed her by accident. His story of the "accident" went something like this. He told police that Heather was being extremely insolent so he had to slap her. She then started laughing at him so he was forced to grab her by the throat to stop her from laughing. He said that unfortunately, he must have grabbed her too tightly because she began to turn blue and stopped breathing. He tried to revive her by putting her in the tub and running cold water on her, but it didn't work.

He then removed her clothes and attempted to put her in a garbage bin, but she didn't fit. Back into the tub she went so he could make her smaller, but he first strangled her with a cord to make sure she was dead. He told police he didn't want to start cutting her up and then have her come alive on him.

He also closed her eyes before he started cutting. He said he couldn't dismember her while she was looking at him. He must have been hearing a strange sound because he told police he found the source of a noise when he cut off her head. He said it was a horrible and unpleasant sound like scrunching. He also said that after cutting her up, she fit quite nicely into the garbage bin.

She was later put in a hole that the West's son, Stephen, had dug with the intention of it becoming a fishpond. Fred put Heather in the hole and built a patio over it. Stephen had unknowingly dug the grave for his own sister's burial.

Police also believed that they killed 15-year-old Mary Bastholm in 1968, though they never found her body. The Wests' son Stephen, later told authorities that he believes Bastholm was one of his father's earlier murders because his father boasted about it.

The Evidence Begins to Surface

Oddly, they violently murdered many of their victims, but then set others free after they had finished using and abusing them. Naturally, some of them went to the police.

The released victims were some extremely lucky women to say the least. Their reports finally got the attention of a Detective Constable named Hazel Savage. Savage was also familiar with Fred West and his arrests for thievery and child molestation through the years since the time he was married to Rena Costello.

Fred videoed an incident in which he raped Anna Marie while Rose held her arms. Anna Marie told friends about her home life who in turn told their parents. This and other information got back to Savage.

This enabled the Detective to obtain a warrant to search the West's property. It was the beginning of the needed evidence to finally remove these damaged and dangerous monsters from the unsuspecting public.

Fred was arrested and charged with rape and sodomy of a minor and Rose for assisting in the rape of a minor. Amazingly, Fred and Rose West were still not suspected of murder. At this time, the younger children were removed from the home.

Due to the evidence found in the home, Detective Savage had the suspicion that there was more going on here and she began digging deeper into this strange family. She had a feeling that there was something suspicious concerning the whereabouts of their daughter Heather and she was determined to find out.

For instance, it was noticed in the videos of the West's and their children that was seized from their home that Heather was never present. Also, in interviews with some of the children, they said something that should not come from the mouths of children.

Apparently, there was a common joke around the West house. Fred told the children that he would buried them under the patio with their sister Heather if they didn't behave.

Unbelievably, the case fell apart when two of the main witnesses decided not to testify. Detective Savage continued questioning the children repeatedly to no avail. Fred and Rose had programmed them and put enough fear in them by then that they would no longer say anything to help the case.

However, the evidence together with case workers reporting the family joke about their sister Heather kept Detective Savage searching. It also appeared that another child, Charmaine, was missing as well. Eventually, Savage put together enough evidence to obtain a warrant to dig on the Wests' property.

Soon after that, Rose answered the door to find the police with warrant in hand. She quickly called Fred to tell him the police were about to dig on their property and they're looking for Heather. It turned out that Fred would be of little help because it took him four hours to get home. He came up with some excuse about passing out due to inhaling paint fumes at work.

Could it have been that Fred was busy disposing of evidence such as fingers and toes or perhaps he had a burial he had not gotten around to completing. That will never be determined.

They began searching the house in addition to excavating the garden in February 24, 1994. The dig was originally intended to search for the body of the daughter Heather, which they soon found. Fred was brought in by the police for questioning the next day. He surprised the police by confessing to the murder of his daughter Heather and he repeatedly told police that Rose knew nothing about it.

Fred and Rose must have been up all that night getting their stories straight. It is thought that Fred assured Rose he would take all the blame and she shouldn't worry. Fred was good to his word, at least in the beginning.

Meanwhile, after the attending pathologist began inspecting the bones of Heather, he brought it to the attention of the police that there was an extra leg bone indicating the presence of at least one other body.

After that discovery, Fred decided he should do some damage control by telling police the location of Alison Chambers and Shirley Robinson's bodies. He hoped this would prevent them from doing any more digging.

It was first thought that Fred did this to avoid being categorized a serial killer, which is someone that kills more than three people. Unbelievably, as it turned out, Fred wanted the police to stop digging because he didn't want his cherished home to be torn apart any further.

Nevertheless, they continued and began to find more human bones. Rose was not arrested until around March 4, 1994. Even then, it was only for sex offenses. Fred had trouble deciding for sure if he wanted to protect Rose after all. He would go on the recant his confession that he killed Heather and then later changed his mind again saying Rose was innocent.

In Britain, prisoners are sometimes assigned an "appropriate adult", which is someone that assists and basically befriends the prisoner. This was normally done for juveniles; however, Janet Leach was assigned to Fred. Leach didn't know she was about to become the confidant of a serial killer.

It turned out that Fred became comfortable enough with Leach that he soon told her the whole gory story. She pointblank asked him if there were more victims. Fred responded that there were six more and went on to draw a sketch of his house and garden complete with the locations of the graves.

Fred knew exactly where they were located; however, he had some trouble remembering all their names. He recalled one that had a scar on her hand; therefore, Scar Hand became her name. Another he called Tulip because he thought she was Dutch, although she was actually Swiss.

Fred was now on a roll and confessed to the murders of his ex-wife Rena Costello and ex-lover, Anne McFall. He told Ieach that he dumped them nearby his childhood home. He then confessed that he buried his step-daughter Charmaine, Fred's child that Rose killed, close to the hotel where they lived in Gloucester. Strangely, Fred would admit to the murders, but he would not admit to the rapes.

Meanwhile, Rose continued to play the role of an innocent woman, denying any involvement in the murders. She went so far as to act horrified at the actions of her perverted husband. When Fred attempted to contact her, she snubbed him not wanting to have anything to do with such a despicable person.

After making bail, Rose moved into a halfway house with her son Stephen and her daughter Mae. The police were not convinced of her innocence and bugged the house. Nevertheless, Rose stuck to it and never spoke of anything that would involve her in murder. Only charges of sexual offense remained against her.

As can be imagined, the town of Gloucester was flooded with the media. The attention had a tremendous impact on the small town. The West's house became known by the appropriate name "The House of Horrors". The residents were in disbelief that this unimaginable crime spree had gone on in their town for 20 years.

The Trial

As it turned out, Fred took the easy way out. He hanged himself in his jail cell by tying together bed sheets leaving Rose to deal with the whole state of affairs.

She was finally charged with 10 of the murders since Rena Costello and Anne McFall were before she was on the scene. She went to trial in October of 1995.

One after another, witnesses took the stand and told their shocking stories. One of the highest drama moments of the trial came with the testimony of Fred's oldest daughter, Anna Marie. She was on the stand for two days. At one point she looked her stepmother straight in the eye as she told a story of sexual abuse and torture that began when she was a little girl of only eight-years-old.

She recalled the incident when she was so savagely raped by her father while Rose held her arms. During the incident, Rose was telling her how lucky she was to have parents to show her how to please her husband when she gets married. She said she was hurt so badly that she couldn't attend school for several days. She also recalled a day that her father strapped her down and raped her while he was home for a quick lunch break. These were only two of the many horror stories she lived.

The second day of her testimony was delayed for several hours because she took an overdose of pills the previous evening.

Another person that offered a wealth of damaging testimony was Fred's *Appropriate Adult* and confidant, Janet Leach. However, she became so stressed that she suffered a stroke during the trial causing another delay. It wasn't until later after the trial's end that Leach could tell police the entire story that Fred confided in her.

One of the key witnesses was Carol Owens who was one of the girls they brought home under the pretense of being a nanny. She was allowed to leave, but only after she endured their sadistic sexual torture. Needless to say, she had tales to tell.

Another witness who is still referred to as Miss A was lured to the West house and saw two naked girls who were being held prisoner. She watched as they were tortured and raped. She was then raped by Fred and sexually assaulted by Rose. She was one of the lucky ones that left that cellar with her life.

It wasn't hard for the jury to come back with a unanimous verdict of guilty on 10 counts of murder. Rose received life in prison.

The Aftermath

The "House of Horrors" at 25 Cromwell Street in Gloucester where nine bodies were found was demolished in October of 1996; however, there seemed to be a curse that affected many of the people associated with Rose and Fred West.

John West, Fred's brother, hanged himself while awaiting his trial for the rape of his own niece Anna Marie.

Anna Marie continued to suffer from the memories of her distorted childhood. In 1999, she attempted suicide by jumping from a bridge. She was rescued, leaving her to live another day with the memory of the horrors from her past.

Stephen West, the son of Rose and Fred, attempted to commit suicide in 2002 in the same manner as his father and uncle by hanging himself. However, it wasn't meant to be because the rope broke.

The actual number of murders will remain a mystery. During his interrogation by the police, Fred stated that there were two more bodies buried in shallow graves that they would never find.

He also told them there were 20 other bodies spread around in various places. He claimed he would show the police the location of one body each year. One wonders if he knew at that time that he would later take his own life and wouldn't be following through with that promise.

Fred took any other secrets he had in his evil little mind with him to his grave. After that, Rose wasn't interested in discussing the matter any further.

According to an article in the DailyMail, dated February 2014, even though Rose West filed for a couple of appeals after she went to prison, she has now decided she never wants to leave her top security jail cell at Low Newton jail in Durham and why would she, her cell is equipped with TV, radio, CD player, and private bathroom. She has never confessed to committing any murders.

Authorities know the women and girls were tortured, raped, killed, dismembered, and buried; however, they don't know the details of many of those crimes. Rose has been asked by numerous people to give those details, but she refuses.

Conclusion

This is an account of actual facts; however, it hard to believe that it's anything other than a fictional horror story.

Even after hearing about the disturbing childhoods of both Rose and Fred West, it's difficult to understand the extent of their warped minds. Even more disturbing is the fact that two people that are this broken can find one another and carry out their evil deeds together.

This story brings us no closer to the answer of what drives serial killers. Both Rose and Fred were abused as children mainly by their fathers; however, it was young women and girls that were the focus of their punishment.

There have been books and a movie made about them to show us how this horrific story unfolds. However, only in our minds can we come close to conjuring up the evil that occurred within the walls of 25 Cromwell Street. We may never know the full extent of the terrors that transpired.

The fact that Fred West is gone and Rose West will never see the light of day should make us all sleep a little more soundly.

www.ingramcontent.com/pod-product-compliance
Lightning Source LLC
Chambersburg PA
CBHW022013150726
47990CB00002B/640